WHAT KIND OF MAN

Also by Tony Gloeggler

ONE ON ONE (Pearl Editions, 1999)

ONE WISH LEFT (Pavement Saw Press, 2002, Second Edition, 2007)

MY OTHER LIFE (Jane Street Press, 2004)

GREATEST HITS (Pudding House Publications, 2009)

THE LAST LIE (NYQ Books, 2010)

TONY COME BACK AUGUST (Bittersweet Editions, 2015)

UNTIL THE LAST LIGHT LEAVES (NYQ Books, 2015)

What Kind of Man

Tony Gloeggler

The New York Quarterly Foundation, Inc.
Beacon, New York

NYQ Books™ is an imprint of The New York Quarterly Foundation, Inc.

The New York Quarterly Foundation, Inc.
P. O. Box 470
Beacon, NY 12508

www.nyq.org

First Edition

Set in New Baskerville

Layout and Design by Raymond P. Hammond

Cover photo by Alexis Rhone Fancher

Library of Congress Control Number: 2020931913

ISBN: 978-1-63045-061-8

What Kind of Man

Acknowledgements

Thank you once again: Raymond Hammond for doing all the work of putting this book together and allowing me and my work to continue to be part of NYQ. Michael Flanagan and Ted Jonathan for closely reading my poems for all these years, for your support and annoying suggestions whenever I thought a poem was perfect.

Thanks for the first time: Bunkong Tuon, that's BK to me, Doug Collura, Michael Mark, John Florio for your thoughts on some of these poems. Alexis Rhone Fancher for the cover photograph and the time you spent on helping me pick the perfect shot. Maria Mazziotti Gillan, Sean Thomas Dougherty, Hayan Charara, and Angelo Verga, poets whose work I admire a great deal, for blurbs saying that these poems do what I worked hard to make them do.

Some of these poems appeared in print: *2 Bridges Review, Asylum, Bogg, The Bridge, Cape Rock, Chiron Review, Commonthought, Echoes, Elysian Fields, Fan, Green Fuse, The Ledge, Liqeuer, Main Street Rag, Mas Tequila Review, Moon City Review, Mudfish, Nerve Cowboy, New Ohio Review, New York Quarterly, Newtown Literary Review, Paterson Literary Review, Pittsburgh Poetry Review, Plainsongs, Poet Lore, Raleigh Review, Rattle, Rhino, Rosebud, San Pedro River Review, Spillway, Turnstile, West Trade Review.*

Autistic Basketball and Good appeared in the anthology *Alongside We Travel/Contemporary Poets on Autism.*

What Kind of Man was nominated for a Pushcart by *New Ohio Review.*

Some appeared online: *Black Coffee Review, B O D Y, Cultural Weekly, Home Planet News, Houseboat, Misfit, Piker Press, Red Fez, Silver Birch Press, Southern Florida Poetry Journal, Trailer Park, Verse Virtual.*

About Time was nominated for a Pushcart by *Cultural Weekly.*

Thanks to all the editors who gave my work a place on their pages.

This one's for my brother Jaime.
Thanks for the kidney and acting like it was nothing

Though we both know you gave me my life back...

Contents

THIS KIND OF ROOM

It's that kind of soft, not too hot, summer day
when all I want to do is be young enough
to run fast break full courts until night falls.
I don't want to subway into the city, stop
in book stores, thumb through bins of used
vinyl for hours, stand in line at the Angelica
for one of those movies where I don't care
if the main character lives or dies. I don't
want to be back in love with Erica, driving
to some quaint upstate town, windows
down, in complete control of the tape deck
and we're both singing along as loud
and as off key as we please: Springsteen,
Beach Boys, old live 1969 Poco. Don't want
to linger over brunch, wander into tiny shops
filled with scented candles and antiques,
not even if we stop at a roadside park,
find a deserted shady spot, spread a blanket
and end up making out like we first met.
I want to be the first and only guy at the schoolyard,
feel the grooves of the ball with my fingertips,
hear it echo off the handball walls, the four
floors of empty brick classrooms, as I take
a few dribbles, make easy lay ups. I don't want
to be in Maine, back in love with Helen
at the Wadleigh Valley county fair watching
Jesse stroke some bored cow, taking pictures
as he rides the long rainbow slide nineteen
straight autistic times no matter how ecstatic
he looks every time. Don't care if he sleeps
through the night and we cuddle through
some video, walk to the bedroom for slow
mind blowing sex and an early morning
rewind. I want to stand at the foul line,
hit a few shots, watch the ball softly fall
through the not yet stolen net. No, not
a little kid on a back in Brooklyn Sunday,

my grandfather, my father, still alive, mom
complaining there's nowhere to place
the lasagna pan and my favorite uncle, Dom,
with his crutches by his side, always saying
*just as long as there's this kind of room
in heaven, we'll all be alright.*' I want to nod
knowingly, maybe slap palms, flick bounce
passes when the other guys start showing up,
talking shit, late night west coast box scores.
I definitely don't want to be sitting inside
at my desk, clicking through emails, reading
about my old schoolyard friend Duden's
kidney transplant and how it all went well,
he's recovering nicely. Don't want to think
about my own kidney condition especially
since it's now official that the medication
didn't work. I don't want to spend a moment
making a list of who would contemplate donating
a kidney for me, who would get sick of visiting
me in the hospital first. Today, all I want to do
is shoot for sides. Duden's my first pick. He grabs
a rebound, hits me with an outlet pass. I glide
down the sideline, cross over, take off and soar
to the hoop. Even if my shot somehow rims, spills
out, the Dude will tip it back in, fill the basket.

RENAL SONOGRAM

Tuesday morning and I'm lifting
my shirt, lying on my back
in a dark room. I have trouble
with the lab technician's accent,
ask her to repeat every question
as she spreads gel on my belly,
presses a wand here and there
taking pictures of my kidneys.

"Please, deep breath." Holding it,
I am hoping for easy answers,
a pill, less sodium in my diet
to stop my calves from swelling
as I sit at my desk writing,
standing and yelling for more
at Los Lobos' Sunday night show.

"No breathing, please." I think
about this morning's email, news
that my oldest friend's nephew
is dead. Thirty-eight years old,
he went to grammar school
with my baby brother. The police
suspect foul play and Kevin's
driving all the way from Cleveland
with his second wife. The wake
will either be a crying, moaning
mess or a half empty room filled
with awkward guilty silence
and I wish I didn't have to go.

"Turn on side, please. Face wall."
After this, I'll ride the G train
to the residence, fire the guy
I was training to help cut
my work load in half. I feel
bad. He's twenty-six, a funny,

ambitious kid who needs money
for his *'baby mama drama.'*
But his attention span's shorter
than a text message
and he kept borrowing cash
from the workers he supervised.

"Lie on back one time again.
Lower pants, please." I undo
my belt, slide my pants down
so the top of my pubic hair
shows. *"Hold breath, please now."*
Younger, I'd have to concentrate,
try hard not to get an erection.
Now, I would be pleased to feel
my cock growing uncontrollably.

I watch the technician carefully
as she ignores me, does her job.
I imagine her hair let loose
from her bun, the lab coat falling
to the floor. But no, she's not
the kind of woman I can picture
working in a Chinatown spa
leading me to the back room.

"Relax. All done, please." I leave
knowing I will have to wait
patiently as possible until next
Tuesday, 12:45, for my doctor
to interpret the results, maybe
look me in the eye and deliver
news I'd never want to hear
or the chance of a happy ending.

THE DIALYSIS SHUFFLE

I settle into my recliner,
my book and iPod to my right,
headphones around my neck.
The technician bundles
my blanket over me.
She then velcros
the blood pressure sleeve
to my left arm, readies the needle
to stab me, hook me up
to dialysis. I nod to the patients
shuffling by for their treatment,
more men than women, more
black than white, some leaning
on crutches, pushing walkers,
most older and worse off
than me. I check the clock,
note when my three hours
will be done. I try to sleep
as long as I can, usually
the first hour and fifteen
minutes, then I pick up
Townie by Andre Dubus,
I am up to the point
where he stops boxing,
writes his first story
and Playboy pays two thousand
for it. Ah, a memoir and fairy tale
all in one. The overhead TVs
are showing *Law and Order,*
The Rifleman or *Married*
With Children. Their voices
collide into gibberish.

A nurse hands me a cold can
of some thick protein drink
that I need help to open.
Vanilla pecan. The nutritionist

goes over my latest blood results,
tells me I'm eating too little
of some things and too much
of everything else. Ninety minutes
to go, I try to fit my headphones
over my head with one hand
and my woolen hat covers
my eyes. I press shuffle, shut
my eyes and turn the volume up.
Music carries me away:

It starts with *Younger Girl*
and I'm thinking the Critters,
but no, it's the Lovin' Spoonful
and I'm walking to Central Park
for John B Sebastian, the night
Thurman Munson's plane crashed
and Erica's hugging me tight
as I try not to believe her.
Surfer Girl. The first song Brian
wrote in his car. He played it
last week at Jones Beach
right after the heavenly
In My Room. I had never
even been to Coney island
when I first heard it
in my father's car. He changed
channels, but already I saw
myself sitting on a blanket
with Claire Kerchoff curled
into my lap expecting Seven
Minutes of Heaven. *Crimson
and Clover* is next, endless
psychedelic shit wafting
from a schoolyard boom box
and I'm running full court
in baggy bell bottoms. Next,
Sam Cooke's too smooth
version of *Havin' A Party*

16

with the relaxed loping beat,
the too syrupy strings
until I remember that first
night I saw Southside,
his Asbury Jukes, encoring
at the Bottom Line, a white
guy showing a black man
how it's done with nothing
but gutter grit and sweat. Ronnie
Spector's beehive bouncing
behind the harmonies, Miami
Steve and the Big Man bumping
rumps as the Professor pounds
the keys and a few years later
Bruce picks up the harmonica
to kick off *The River* at No Nukes,
that mourning, moaning opening
about a life closing in on itself.
The band joins in, drives it
to the reservoir, lifts it with memories
full of possibilities until I'm singing
along, kicking my feet when
a LeBron James cramp
grabs my calf and I'm screaming
like a banshee, a *Spirit*
In The Night, as two nurses
rush over, help me stand
tall. Press down. Hard.
Walk. No shuffling allowed,
back to the real world,
eyes wide open with tubes,
needles dangling from my arms.

A LITTLE MUSIC

Abby, your technician
for today's treatment, hums
a gospel song as she sticks
the needles in the crook
of your elbow, attaches you,
the tubes, to the dialysis
machine and sets it
for three and a half hours
when the floor nurse walks by.
She squeezes her shoulder, offers
her condolences, starts whispering
about her son's memorial day.
How long has it been, she asks,
and Abby says she's just trying
to make it through the shift
and not think too much.
Hopefully, she can reach
the cemetery before it closes,
stop at the florist in time to buy
fresh flowers. You lie there
wondering if you should say
something, try to express
how sorry you feel for her
or whether this was something
she wouldn't want you
to know, something she wishes
you never overheard. You roll
the front of your wool hat
over your eyes, fit headphones
over your ears and hope
to drop off to sleep. You wonder
what happened to her son
and you leaf through newspaper
headlines: shot by a white cop
in a store front robbery,
a gang member's stray bullet
from the back seat of a car,

18

a roof top sniper shooting
a raw recruit in an unwinnable
war, an infant smothered
in his sleep. Always, too young
to die. When you open
your eyes, Abby is punching
buttons on the computer
next to you checking blood
pressure, your water levels.
You press the pause button,
hear she is humming
the same song. She apologizes
for making too much noise
and waking you. She talks
about a few years ago when soft
jazz played through the speakers
until a few patients complained.
She points them out, names
names and you feel relieved,
knowing you would never
be on that list. *You know,*
she says, *a little music*
makes the day go faster,
smoother. You grab
your iPod, nod and wave
for her to lean closer.
You lift the headphones
off your head, hand them to her.
Carefully, she nestles them
on the top of her new hairdo,
fits them over her ears. Press
the button. Monk's *Bemsha*
Swings. She closes her eyes
and her head sways, gently,
like a flower with morning
mist lifting from her eyes.

SONG OF SOLOMON

Today. When your hands first
lift out of pockets, pop
open coat buttons, swing
arms lightly by your side,
you forget it's Wednesday
in February. You put a dollar
in the homeless guy's hand, grab
today's paper off the stand, walk
down subway stairs. Today,
the F train sits in the station,
waits patiently for you. You lean
against closed doors, unfold
the paper to spring training.
Gleyber Torres, this year's prize
prospect, kneels on deck,
swings a weighted bat, stares
past the center field fence.
CC twirls, throws in the bull
pen, hopes to squeeze one more
season out of his left arm. Today
you believe they'll both make it.

You lift your head, leave
Florida and discover a young
woman sitting across the car.
Long fingers push loose curls
of dark hair from her eyes, turn
and dance through pages of *Song
of Solomon*. The words brush
her lips, brighten brown eyes
with tinges of green. You want
to take her hand, get off the next
stop, rent a red corvette and gas it
up. She'll glide across the seat,
fit under your arm. The radio
will sing *Sweet Soul Music*,
you'll roll windows down as wheels

kick up speed. Today she lifts
her eyes, finds yours and touches
you with the softest smile. You watch
her stand, step off at West Fourth.
And today, she turns, looks back,
holds you all the way to Brooklyn.

BEACH BOY

Before you found yourself
sitting with your eyes shut,
lifting closer to heaven
as your headphones poured
Pet Sounds into your ears,
you sat in the back seat
while your dad drove slowly
through town, his left arm
dangling out the rolled down
window holding a cigarette.
You hoped he would turn
on the radio, quickly tire
of the all news station
and switch to the *good guys*
on WMCA, counting the top ten
down to *Help Me, Rhonda.*

Your fingers drum lightly
against your thighs,
you mouth along the words
to the chorus. Stopping
at the next corner, girls
from your fifth grade class
cross the street, wave thanks.
As the guitar fades away,
your father glances
in the rear view mirror,
watches your head move,
follow Claire and her cut offs
turn the corner. He catches
your eye and nods
as if he knows something
you still hadn't figured out.

45 RPMS

ANGIE'S PIZZA after school.
The juke box scratches out
the Stones. We order two
slices, a large Coke. You
blow smoke rings in my ear,
leave pink lipstick on crushed
butts. I eat your crust,
finger pick guitar riffs,
sing, "*Ti-i-ime is on my side,
yes it is.*" Angie yells,
"*Shut the hell up back there.*"
We get up, buy a lemon ice,
take turns licking it
slowly down Main Street.

INDEPENDENCE DAY

As soon as you hear
Federici's organ moaning
deep down in your bones
punctuated by The Professor's
piano, you can see Bruce
with his head hung low
lurking in the shadows
still steps from the microphone.
When he moves closer
the crowd rumbles, roars
and Springsteen shushes
them quiet with his hands.
He folds both hands over
the mic, opens his mouth
and his hoarse whisper
reigns over the arena.
Instantly you're taken
home, all the way back
to the house you grew
up in, walking the dark
hallway past your parents'
bedroom after another
aimless late night.

Happy to have avoided
seeing your father
all day, you heard him
talking to your mom,
his voice a simmering
whisper, telling her
how sick and tired
he was of you. *When
will he get a freakin' job
and move his lazy ass out?*
Your mom listened, waited
until he ran out of breath,

just give him a little more
time. He's my son too
and I won't let you
throw him out. No, never.

Your father never had any
time, he quit school at twelve
to work on an ice truck
during the tail end
of the depression. He married
your mom at nineteen, nine
months later they had you
and for eight hours a day,
plus all the overtime
he could get, every damn day,
he worked at the A&P warehouse
trying to stretch his money
to the next pay check.
You were floundering
around in college, reading
novels and sociology textbooks
trying to find some kind
of work you wouldn't hate
with every breath. You spent
most of your time in schoolyards
shooting hoops, leaning
on the hood of your car
trying to talk Julia Jordan
into a ride along the shore.

You walked to your room,
dropped your clothes on the floor,
got into bed without waking
your brother and you wish
you had known how to thank
him for that time back then,
that chance to find yourself
and a job with some sense

of purpose and contentment,
but all he ever did was yell
and criticize anyway. You fall
asleep humming along
to the song you swear Springsteen
wrote about you and your father,
"They ain't gonna do to me
what I watched them do to you."

MOTHER'S DAY

When I mention I ran into a cousin
I hadn't seen in twenty years,
my mother tells me the last time
she saw Michael his kids were
"what do you call them
with all those tattoos and pins
sticking in and out of their noses
and eyelids, thick black make up
streaking down their cheeks…"
Some other cousin said his daughter
turned out to be a lesbian and lives
somewhere in the Poconos
with her girlfriend. She says
Michael never talks about her,
pretends she doesn't exist.
She heard she's thin, a beautiful
tall blonde, a dealer. She laughs
and waves her hand at me,
"No, you idiot, not drugs,
she works at the local casino."

Unfortunately, I never met her
or her girlfriend and my mother
doesn't offer any updated photos
so I can't fill my thoughts with exciting,
made-for-my-own-personal-use
porn. Instead, I listen to my mom
rattle on and on about my cousins,
their marriages, births, lingering
diseases. When she finally stops
to take a breath, I ask if she thinks
Michael's daughter is happy,
Without thinking, she answers,
"I hope so" and I was reminded
how I always knew my mother
would love me whoever
I turned out to be, no matter

what dumb disastrous destructive
things I'd ever do and I'm still
not sure how good or bad
this should make me feel,
only that I often wonder
if I could ever feel that way
about anybody and if that's
what's most wrong with me.

ACCOUNTING

Paying bills at the end
of the month, I think about
my mom sitting at the kitchen
counter, my father pacing
behind her as I sat cross-legged
in front of the black and white
waiting for Ed Sullivan to get
through the magicians and acrobats,
finally bring on The Rolling Stones,
The Rascals. He did all the math,
adding, subtracting, dividing
in his head. She did all the writing
in a neat flowing script that danced
across the check, her signature
a pirouette. Round and round
they went as cigarette smoke
swirled to the ceiling, which ones
could wait, which ones had to be paid
yesterday. Mortgage, station wagon,
three kids in Catholic School
on a 40 hour a week warehouse job
plus all the overtime he could get.

Me, I live in a rent stabilized
apartment, no wife, kids or car.
Not rich, I make more money
than I need, pay everything
as soon as it's due. I could travel
anywhere, retire anytime
and sometimes I wonder
what they think of my life.
But my father's dead, my mom
wouldn't tell me the truth
and I try not to think too long
about what I might be missing.

LEGACY

If I didn't force myself
to get out of bed, answer
the phone this Saturday
afternoon, the anniversary
of my father's death
might have passed me by
unnoticed again. My baby
brother invited us all over
for Sunday dinner,
my other brother
will probably go
to the cemetery instead.
He'll place sunglasses
and recent pictures
of the grand kids
my father never knew
on the head stone and pray
no one will steal them.
I remember dropping
a fistful of dirt in the ground,
hoping to help fill the hole
and how hard I tried to stop
crying. As I walked back
to the car, my mother's
younger, sexiest friend
hugged me, whispered
I was always her favorite.
I still wonder if Brenda
meant anything by that.

The next time I'll go back
is when my mom dies. Sorry,
but I don't believe in that kind
of thing and I can't even say
I think of my father regularly.
When my family talks
about him, they only mention

happy or funny moments
while our nagging conflicts,
his limitations and blind spots
stick with me more. Whenever
I bring any of that up,
the room grows all quiet.
I do miss him, but the world
would not be any easier
if he lived longer. Mostly
I realize I am more like him
than anybody else and nothing
anyone says will change that.

FATHER'S DAY

I know I'm not the one
that should say this
but the world could use
more men like me.
Like everything else,
I will say it softly
while I look in your eyes
and you may even
need to move closer
to hear.
            You'll know
it is the truth
because my father
taught me to say
what I think and feel
and then do my best
to live it every day,
and since he died
years ago too soon
it is left to me.

FAMILY

Sitting around the dinner table,
I imagine you've wondered,
once or twice, every night,
whether you were adopted?
Maybe a bored, over worked nurse
placed you in the wrong crib
the evening you were pried
out of your mother's belly.
Your father could have found you
on an upstate hunting trip
at the mouth of a river nestled
in a basket, or some terrified
fifteen year old girl wrapped
you in a navy blue sweat shirt
and left you on the back porch
next to bundles of tied together
newspapers. They took you in,
looked at you as a gift or burden
from god and did their best
to nurture you, torture you
in the name of love and family.

Even during today's Sunday
visit, look to your left, the right,
across the table. If you take
a deep enough breath, the smell
of pot is a fog rising off your sister's
tan wrinkled skin. Your brother
holds forth like Archie Bunker's
mentor on sports and race,
celebrity gossip, his five
fucking cats. And god bless
your baby brother, his wife,
two adorable young kids,
working too many hours
downtown in a corner office
overlooking the construction

of The Freedom Tower in risk
management and rooting
for the Yankees, checking
his cell phone every few minutes
to keep track of fantasy leagues.

But you, you're the weird one,
too quiet, with your writing
and reading, alone, no new
girlfriend, that autistic kid
you still visit in Maine
and now this kidney condition
that you don't like talking about.
Except the medication didn't help
and you will eventually, inevitably
need a transplant and siblings
have the best chance of matching.
Using your distant, measured news
caster voice, you recite the facts,
describe the procedure, the risks,
success rate and after care, hope
that one of them will love you
enough or feel obligated enough
to consider it and step forward,
help you maybe live a little longer.

GOD'S GIFTS

It's the kind of day that feels like a gift
from God. An early April morning
with temperatures already flirting
with sixty degrees. Bright blue skies,
a few wispy clouds and a whisper
of breeze lifting the short skirts
of women that make you want to sing
hymns of praise. One of those days
you can't resist, a day that forces you
to cut class or call out from work
so you can spread a newspaper
across a table at the corner café.
Waiting for pancakes, sunny
side eggs, you turn to sports,
believe all the Yankee veterans
will have one more injury free year
and their prize prospect will exceed
every bit of hype. Later, you'll walk
to the schoolyard, get picked for a three
on three. You are totally unstoppable
and your squad streaks to a string
of six straight wins. You call Suzanne
who says she can get away, meet you
by Prospect Park. You stroll along
holding hands, stop for soft serve
ice cream with sprinkles and lick
the slow drippings off of each other's
fingers, spread a blanket behind a bunch
of bushes and make out. Coming up
for air, she promises to leave her husband.

But no, today you are waiting for the late
as always Access-A-Ride to drive you
to dialysis. You'll sit in the waiting room,
listen for your mispronounced name
to come through the speakers. You'll lie
back while the machine removes liquid,

35

filters your blood for three hours as you try
to fall asleep, but can't. You feel colder
and colder and closer to cramping
as you watch the clock creep forward,
the orderlies lift the one-legged woman
into her wheelchair. Home, you fix a bland,
tasteless lunch, drink a few sips of water,
limp to your bedroom and let your clothes
drop down to the floor. You nap restlessly,
dream of a smiling Suzanne, happily married,
living in Austin with two kids. You wake up
with a splitting headache in time to catch
the Yankee game. Five games under .500,
their starting pitcher gives up a first inning,
two out, three run homer and they helplessly
keep leaving runners on base as the game
grinds on. Between pitches, you remind
yourself that dialysis is keeping you alive,
and that you are happy not to be dead yet
as you pray for one full night of sleep.

9-1-1

The flashing red lights splash
against the brick buildings
as medics wheel the stretcher
to the curb. I take a peek,
the man looks a lot like me
and I wonder how they opened
my door, who called 9-1-1. Maybe
the super noticed my overflowing
mail box, the newspapers piled
on my welcome mat, and he rang
my bell and got no answer
a few times. Did they find me
lying in bed, my underwear bunched
around my ankles or my body
folded over the toilet bowl?
Did they notice the bare walls,
too many books, too many CDs
and my desk covered with scattered
papers? Nod at the open pill bottles
strewn upon the kitchen counter?
Shake their heads as fluffs of dust
blew across the floor, dirty dishes
soaked in the sink, shirts hung
from every door knob and think
I was too sick to take care of myself
or guess I was always kind of lazy,
a bit of a slob? Did they stop and look
at the photos on the bulletin board:
three old girl friends who loved me
and left, came back years later
and left me again, Larry
with his down syndrome tongue
hanging out of his open mouth
and raising his arms like he kicked
the Super Bowl's winning field goal
after getting a yellow ribbon
for taking part in Special Olympics

and that one of me holding Jesse,
upside down by his ankles,
six years old with his smile
as wide as a basketball court,
his hair flopped out like Pistol
Pete Maravich and my mom,
dad and Jaime looking all stiff
and serious, uncomfortable as hell
while the photographer took
too long to shoot? Did they find
my hidden bottle of quarters,
were they tempted to pocket
a handful? Was my computer
sleeping or open to a porn site,
the Yankees' late night box score,
my last poem, nearly finished?

NAM

I watched
The 11 o'clock news
All the way through
On a school night
To watch James Greene
Roll down the screen
With this week's dead

Jimmy
Who lifted me
On his shoulders
And held me there
While I fastened
The net's white loops
Tightly on his new
Backyard hoop

THREE SPEED

You walked home slowly, trying
to find words to tell your father
your new three speed was stolen.
You had pedaled past the overgrown
lots, the dumping grounds, all
the way to the new soccer field
at the edge of your neighborhood.
You and John Calamari stayed late,
took turns kicking field goals
through uprights. Riding home
on the narrow path, three older
kids ambushed you, pulled you
to the ground, punched, stomped.
You stopped fighting back when
one kid pulled a knife. A few
more kicks and they were gone,
racing away in the opposite direction.

Cal somehow got away, only lost
his football, which made you
feel worse, slower, dumber
and weaker than him. Home,
your father yelled *what the hell
were you doing over there, letting
them take your bike like that.*
There were no good answers
and you knew he was right.
His face muscles tightened,
the strain spread down his neck,
to his arms, into his right hand.
He smacked you once, twice
and you knew enough to quietly
take it. After doing what
he thought a father should,
you both sat down to dinner
and he sort of apologized,
saying how it was just a bicycle,
maybe you'd get a new one
for Christmas, your birthday.

SHOTGUN

I was one of the stars
of my Catholic high school
baseball team. Riding shotgun
on our way to an away game,
I ignored the song on the radio,
closed my eyes and imagined
my high kick wind-up, the ball
exploding out of my hand, flying
past the batter's too late swing
in cartoon colors when Doug Dwyer
grabbed the hair hanging down
my neck and yelled in a John Wayne
kind of drawl *let's round us up
some long haired Jews and fags
and kick some ass.* I shook my head,
mumbled *let's grab us some spics
and niggers too* when I realized
Billy Mitchell, one of the half dozen
black kids in the school, was sitting
behind me. Everything blurred
and the song on the radio began
to bend, fade farther away, as I felt
red heat creep up my and reach
my face. Turning as fast as I could,
I said that I didn't mean anything
by it, that I was only joking, shit
I'm sorry. Billy didn't say a thing,
didn't shrug or nod. He kept staring
out the window. Finally, I did too,
trying to find the world he lived in.

POST OFFICE

Like Charles Bukowski, I worked
in the post office. Cousin Louie
set up a special appointment
and they hired me immediately
during the Christmas rush.
I couldn't take it, half sitting
on this slanted chair in front
of a boxed-in cubicle, sliding
envelopes into zip coded slots
as some half wit strutted down
the aisles telling me to speed
things up, stop talking and keep
one foot on the floor at all times.
I wanted to tell him to go fuck
himself, but my mom was working
a few aisles over trying to make
extra money. At our lunch break,
I told her I was quitting. We split
a meatball hero and I leaned
over, kissed her goodbye,
waited for the elevator.

I wasn't hearing any muses
or believed I was meant
to be a writer or anything
like that. It just sucked
and I didn't need money
that bad. My father wanted me
to walk to cousin Louie's,
apologize. I told him no,
that I didn't like him.
Hard to believe he didn't
smack me around a bit,
grab me by the neck
and drag me over there.
I finished high school,
killed six years in college,

completed a silly degree
and miraculously fell
into a job I still love.

Bukowski eventually quit
the post office, became
a celebrated poet, played
his rebel drunk persona
to the hilt. Me, I write too.
No drinking, no drugging
and I've fucked too few
women. Thousands idolize
and imitate him. Hardly
anyone reads my work.
But that's not what this poem
is trying to be about. It's about
my mom and how she lasted
the whole month through
and that Christmas morning,
1970, when I unwrapped my gifts
and opened every Dylan album,
Freewheelin', Blonde On Blonde,
Bringing it All Back Home, John
Wesley Harding, Highway 61,
Nashville Skyline, Another Side,
even god damn *Self Portrait.*

QUEENS NY 1979

Just another summery spring morning in May and I'm sitting
on my stoop, tightening the laces on my high-tops. My mom yells,
tells me to be home for supper. I pretend not to hear, dribble my way
across the street, up the black paved path to the courts. Usually
I'm there before anyone else, working on my left hand, perfecting
bank shots, running an imaginary full speed full court game, stopping
and popping jump shots with Marv Albert's *"Yes, and it counts"*
bursting in my brain. But today, the school janitors Ernie and Lopez
are out with brushes and buckets whitewashing the handball wall,
methodically working from left to right, covering some writing,
some drawings, that look like primitive cave paintings of stick figures
in chains getting on boats to sail to the other end of the wall
where a distorted map of Africa sits under big black block letters
dripping, shouting, NIGERS GO HOME, with only one fucking G.

I quit dribbling and Lopez, a guy who sneaks me in the gym
on winter nights and keeps telling me in loud Muhammad Ali
motor mouth style how he'll beat my butt in paddle ball,
gives me a look, shakes his head slowly. I wish I could say
something like couldn't they have at least spelled the god
damn word right and laughed together at their stupidity.
But he is a dark skinned man and I am a seventeen year old
white boy who live and die in separate worlds. I fast break
to the far court, stand at the foul line with the ball resting
on my hip, hoping he knows it wasn't me and wondering
what I would have done if I had been there with all my friends,
too much beer. Picked up a basketball, took shots in the dark
while everyone wrote on the wall? Walked home all alone?
But I know, even now, I might not have the balls to stop them.

12/8/80

I can't remember what we ate
or anything we talked about
as you and your sister sat
on our ugly pillow couch,
lifted gas station giveaway
glasses filled with cheap wine
to your lips. I sat with my legs
folded indian-style on the floor,
back pressed flat against
the base, my head between
your legs while you knitted
my hair into two loose braids.
I don't remember music,
but I can easily hear Van
or Ralph McTell playing.
It was nearing midnight. Wind
blown snow was falling harder,
starting to cover the streets.
We found extra blankets, sheets,
gave up one of our pillows
to make Dana's night as cozy
as possible. You followed me
into the bedroom. We had only
been living together for a month
and I watched you undress,
slip under the comforter, fit
into a fetal position, burrow
into me and whisper something
about tonight being the kind
of night that made getting old
at twenty-five seem nearly
bearable. I kissed your neck,
never thinking about Dana's
long, wrap-around legs,
her excited eyes always
hinting she was up for anything.
You reached behind, found

my cock and brought it to life.
When I pulled you close,
you were already wet.
I remember everything
growing quiet, the world
slowing down, settling
into one sweet moment.

That morning, you and Dana
had early classes. Working
an afternoon shift, I was still
lying in bed, trying to find
a few more hours of sleep
when you came in crying.
The radio was playing Beatle
songs, cuts from *Double
Fantasy* and when the set
ended, the DJs voice broke in,
hushed and deep, saying
John Lennon was dead,
killed last night by a gunman.
You came back to bed and Dana
joined us. No one said anything
and we stayed there for maybe
fifteen minutes. While Lennon
and The Beatles never meant
to me what he meant to the rest
of the world, you loved him,
his music, and sometimes
I still miss you and I'll never
forget where I was and who
I was in love with the night
John Lennon died.

NEIGHBORHOOD KIDS

Ed's new wife wants to know
what he was like as a kid.
I have no idea. All I remember
is he was ten and I was eight
and we spent every summer day
playing stickball in the street
or wiffle ball in my driveway.
His favorite memory is a weekday
morning, waking at 5:00 AM,
him, my father and me taking
the 6 train, the view of Yankee
Stadium pulling into the station,
waiting in line for hours to sit
in the bleachers and watch
the Yankees and Giants play
the third game of the '62 Series.
I remember pitching, winning
the CYO sixth grade championship
while he batted clean-up.

Ed hurt his arm, quit baseball
in high school. He was the first
neighborhood kid who grew
his hair long. He wore frilly,
dashikis and walked quickly
past my stoop with his head down.
All the moms and dads whispered
about drugs and fags, wondered
what the hell was wrong with him.
My father, who never let me grow
my hair, would nod and repeat
no, he's a good kid. Ed played
the B3 organ like Felix Cavaliere
of The Rascals as girls pressed
closer to the stage, yelled his name.
If I wasn't so self absorbed
in my own schoolyard glories,

I probably would have looked up
to him, wanted to be him. Later,
I played softball with his younger
brothers, my mom would see
his mother at church and I'd catch
news flashes: law school, wild
dangling curls, long black coat,
his conversion to Orthodox Judaism,
married, rich, three kids, estranged
from his parents, eventually divorced,
leaving the Hasidic community
for tailored suits, an Upper East Side
condo, perfectly trimmed wispy hair.

Last Thursday we drove to see
the Rascals reunion. Forty years
since they last played together
with Felix singing sweet, more soulful
than any white man should be allowed.
Dino twirling his sticks, pounding
the beat like 1968. Driving home,
we talked about Catholic school,
memorizing catechism that left
no room for discussion or doubt.
The way we did anything
our fathers told us and how
they hit us when we didn't
do them fast enough. All the things
no one ever talked about, things
that haunt us most. His first girl
friend's suicide. The Sunday night
my cousin Jimmy shot-gunned
his brains across his bedroom.
His father changing their name
from Davidowitz to Davis.
My mother never answering
any questions about her mother,
never wondering why she left,
why my grandfather kicked her

out of the house, why my mom
hung up whenever she called
late at night, never caring
to listen, not one thread
of wonder, too afraid to hear
anything but the version
her father fed her, the one
that held her life together.

LUCK

Surprised by the bright redness
idling in my driveway, I breathe
the new car smell in as I strap
the seat belt around me, latch it.
My younger brother's behind
the wheel, back on the road
again. It could be 25 years ago,
any softball Sunday morning.
Except he's not hung over
and there's no beer can sweating
between his thighs. The same
forties music that played
from Grandpa's kitchen radio
swings from the speakers,
the Andrews Sisters singing
about apple trees, boys
coming home safe and soon.
I almost say something sarcastic
about picking the music
since I lent him the money
to buy this car, but I promised
myself I'd keep quiet. John
has thanked me too many
times already and I'm happy
he's somehow stopped drinking
without any help from a higher
power. Since we put the bats
and balls away, he's grown louder
and louder about Trump and Hillary,
immigration and witch hunts,
the way our youngest brother
is raising his kids without religion.

When this beeping sound starts,
he shakes his head, grabs
the breathalyzer and blows
into it like he's trying to stretch

50

a single into a double
until red letters slide across
the tiny screen, telling him
he *passes* so he's free to keep
driving and begin complaining
about the damn thing going
crazy every ten minutes,
how it makes him take his eyes
off the road, the skyscraping cost
of his insurance, the nearly nine
years his license was suspended
when I reach for the radio
hoping to find a summer song
filled with sunlight or some
loud annoying announcer
going on and on about John
and his blessed good luck,
how he never killed anyone
the hundreds of times he drove
drunk, until he finally shuts up.

AU REVOIR LES ENFANTS

After the movie
I said I would do
all I could

Hide you
under my bed
bring you
bread and wine
guide you
past guarded borders

I would do that
for you, for
anyone

But if black boots
kicked in the door, pressed
a gun to my temple,
said, *where's the Jew*
my mouth would open
point a finger

And I would breathe
deep, glad to be alive
for one more moment

BEFORE

Yes, that summer. 1979. The one
before we moved in together.
You rented a one bedroom
in Forest Hills and I played
full court all day, ate at my mom's
then biked to your place. Suspended
between growing up and the kid
I wanted to remain, I sometimes
stayed the night. The morning songs
of the Hebrew camp two yards away
woke us and I hurried, tried
to come one more time before
your alarm clock sounded. I'd watch
you dress for work, a counselor
for a woman's health clinic
run by a crazy lady who preached
the politics you believed in. Sometimes,
you'd invite your friends, your sisters,
over for dinner and we'd sit around
the table. To delay cleaning up,
I'd half listen to the conversation
and try to find a slot to fit
a word or two in. Maybe music.
Or maybe I'd play poet, mention
a poem I was working on, one
I wasn't sure was ready for your eyes,
your fingers to lift from my notebook,
type onto a blank page and make it
official. Sometimes, you'd drive me
home. We'd sit at the curb until the sun
came up and my father stepped out
of the door on his way to a job
he hated as we held our breath,
held in our smiles and he pretended
not to want to kill us. Yes, before
I started working a job I'd love.
Before I learned how little
I knew about loving someone.
Before I knew I should do anything
to somehow hold you in my life.

POET

The first time anyone
said my name and used
the word poet next to it
was in the early nineties.
I was part of William Packard's
workshop and after class
he told me about this reading
celebrating New York Quarterly's
30th anniversary. He declared
in his booming Orson Welles voice
that I would read one poem
and even if he badly needed
a shower with seven vestal
virgins scrubbing away, I knew
I couldn't, wouldn't say no.

I dressed in my best black jeans
and faded denim shirt, found
the room in the NYU library
and pointed at my name
on the flyer when the pristine
woman at the door asked me
for 10 dollars. I would read
somewhere in the middle,
between Michael Moriarty
and Amari Baraka and already
I was nervous, trying to sneak
glances at the spiral notepaper
my poem was scribbled on.

Moriarty read in the voice
he saved for Shakespeare
or the sermon on the mount
and I expected the cheese
and crackers to turn into steak
and lobster. No, I can't say
I understood what his poem
was trying to be about, but back
home I started watching Law

and Order religiously. Baraka's
spit flew through his fifteen
minute rant and he grew
blacker and angrier by the line.
An elegant woman pronounced
my name wrong and described me
as the kind of young, promising poet
who would help The New York Quarterly
move its future in the right direction

My poem was twenty-five
bare boned lines, without a rhyme
or metaphor in sight, spoken
in plain every day language
about my father. Dinner
was winding down, him
and me were the only ones
left at the table. He changed
chairs, hunched closer to me
and told me they were cutting
back at the factory. He was fifty
years old and if he lost his job
he wouldn't know what to do.

My father would never say
anything like that to anyone
and I just looked at him
until he got up and went
into the living room. I read
in a too low voice that seemed
to be hoping to crack and act
like some kind of man. After,
I thought some girls would talk
to me, tell me how deeply
my poem moved them
as they touched my arm
and said they'd love
to see all of my work,
but their fathers were not
like mine and no I'd never
be the kind of guy

they'd either take home
for one regrettable night
or to meet their mom.
Instead, I drank a little
more wine, thanked Packard
for including me and took
the subway back to Flushing,
the place where I belonged.

I tried to read my book, but kept
thinking about what it meant
being a poet. Mostly I was glad
no one I knew and hung out with
suspected I could spend hours
in my room writing and cutting
my poems down to size. No one
would call me a faggy artist,
ask me to stand on a car hood
and start rhyming when the night
got long and everyone grew
bored with everything and still
were too scared to head home
to our ever shrinking lives.
But deep down, I felt sure,
if I ever met Moriarty and Baraka
in a late night alley, my poem
would kick both of their poems' asses
with its hands tied behind its back.

WEDDING

This summer, I went to a Jewish
wedding at a winery. Of course
I thought of you. It was warm,
sunny and most of the men wore
yarmulkes. The women carried
parasols. I was dressed in my best
black jeans, a dark sports jacket
and no tie. You would have probably
carried one in your bag, tied it
around my neck in the car
and I would have complained
all day. The rabbi was short, stubby
and talked too long. The groom,
my first boyhood Flushing friend
stepped on a wine glass
and *Wouldn't It Be Nice*
played as he kissed the bride
and they strolled down the aisle.

You would have remembered
our first date. Jesse Colin Young
had cancelled and we ate Italian
food in the Village. Too early to end
the evening and both of us living
with our parents, we went back
to my house, my basement room.
I put on *Pet Sounds*, played *Surf's
Up* a few times to show you why
I liked The Beach Boys better
than the Beatles and you should
too. I walked you home, not holding
hands. Our shoulders touched,
I think, accidentally. At your door,
you leaned closer, kissed me
with a tint of tongue. Surprised
and not knowing what to do
with my hands, I squeezed

your ass with my right hand
once. You didn't mind, maybe
even, I hoped, pulled me closer.

I didn't know anybody except
the couple, his mom and younger
brothers and we talked about
our schoolyard superstar days,
told stories about our dead fathers.
Maybe you would have mentioned
your sister's wedding, back
when we were living together,
whether I could attend or not,
how I would be introduced,
the never talked about, non-Jew
you loved, where I would sit
and eat, what I might say. Really,
I never wanted to go, but felt
I should be there, that I belonged
with you. Happy to stay home
that day, I played a softball
double header, ate meat balls
at my mom's. When she asked
about you, I explained about
the wedding, the complications.
I could tell she was offended
as she walked toward the oven
and instantly, almost innocently,
said that they were the Jewish ones.

The band played Motown soul
only crunchier. No, I still
can't dance; but I imagined you
gracefully translating ancient
Grateful Dead-head sways and twirls
into classic R&B white girl grooves.
And yes, I would have danced the slow
ones with you. We'd both remember
the one time you talked about getting

married. Lying in bed, I was happy,
completely in love, expecting to stay
that way and didn't see any reason
to change a thing, deal with our families.
Maybe we'd wonder why we never
talked about it again. Or maybe
I wouldn't be thinking at all.
I'd just hold you tight, shut
my eyes, and let you lead me
wherever you wanted to go.

KINDS OF BLUE

Outside your window
it's all day rain, you drop
the needle on vinyl and each
breath of Miles' horn colors
your soul all blue as you sit
at your desk and read about
Robin Williams killing himself
all over the internet: his gifts
and talents, how much
he meant to the world,
his warmth and generosity,
that photo he posted
on his daughter's 25th birthday,
the sadness and anger people
feel for his loss and you're surprised
how much it touches you. Yes,
you will still pause any time
you click through countless
cable stations and stumble
upon one of the few movies
of his you loved. You will miss
every fifteen minute, manic,
machine gun fire monologue
filled with his assorted
accents and scattered
associations as he plugs
his latest mediocre movie
to some stunned talk show
host who could only dream
of being as quick and funny.

But mostly, you thought
of your friend in Virginia,
how nearly three weeks
have passed since you heard
from him. Too often, his silence
means that he's too busy

watching over and taking care
of his daughter, that dealing
with the hopelessness of depression
is overwhelming her again
and the fear she will never
feel nearly normal, halfway
happy to be alive, is burrowing
into her every sensation
and he doesn't know
if he can take much more.

You think of your recent
open heart surgery, the slow
recovery that feels like stagnation,
your impending kidney transplant,
the struggle to climb a flight
of subway stairs, the rotting
tinny taste embedded in dark
caverns of your throat,
the deep belches and retches
as you swallow your pills
and you feel sure your balls
are gonna shoot out of your mouth,
roll across the floor and you'll
try to bend down, pick them up
and carefully place them back
in their sack. But no, even if
your best days are far behind,
that every little thing you do
may always be a graceless,
tedious chore and you can barely
imagine anyone holding you
through a winter's night, not once
have you wanted to fall asleep
and never wake up. You worry
about the next time you talk
to your friend, wonder what
you could ever say, knowing
he will never take one easy
breath, sleep restfully again.

BED TIME

She can't sleep, keeps
getting up to check
window locks, door
knobs, sits in the kitchen,
smokes cigarettes. Back
in bed, she wraps both
arms around her knees,
clenches them tight
to her chest. He reaches
for the light. She turns
away and he starts
to stroke her hair.
She tells him to stop,
please. He's sorry, asks
can he hold her.
She breathes deep, feels
his arms around her

And she tastes the leather gloved hand
strapped across her mouth again. Her face
slams against the garage wall and that voice
hisses *don't make a sound* as he tugs and tears
at her clothes. He shoves a knee between her legs,
spreads her thighs wider with a fist. His cock
rips her open, pumps harder and faster, spits
inside her with a shudder. He steps back, starts
to run and her mouth yells and yells and yells

For help. He brings
her closer, holds her,
softly, whispers
it's alright darlin',
sshh, try to sleep.
He rocks her slowly.
She tries to shut
her eyes, feels
his cock pressed
against her ass.

THOSE THREE YEARS

Did you love me forever
Just for those three days?
　　　　　—Lucinda Williams

I know, you've heard it all
before. She was twenty-four,
unsure, impressionable, unhappy
and unaware of her own truth
and beauty. Me, mid-forties,
a mentor helping her in a new
job. Trainings, meetings, lunches,
a Special Olympics picnic, holiday
office party, strings of emails,
a home phone call the night
after Christmas, a Brooklyn
walk in snowfall all the way
to my couch, my bed. Add
her long time, inattentive,
live-in boyfriend, my freshly
torn apart heart and you
can roll your eyes now.

But I never did anything
like that before or since
and from the first time
she sat in my office going
over budgets, payroll forms
and she laughed when I told her
to never read the regulations,
they can only get in the way,
it felt like a swarm of bees
bumping and buzzing against
our skin. How every
time she started to leave,
one more question rolled
out of her lovely mouth.

We both slowly, started
to use the word love
between the words I

and you, and I believed
it was true. It stayed that way
two, three times a week
for three years. Her rushing
home, her boyfriend once
wondering why her blouse
was on backwards, my hand
beneath her dress in the back
row of a matinee movie,
a parked car blow job outside
the fire house around the block
from her place, the sirens
and lights bursting out
of the driveway a second
before I came, driving home
from a New Jersey concert
the night all the lights went out
on the east coast, driving over
the dark deserted bridge, the radio
hushed, her and me the only ones
on the road, the only ones alive,
ready to start a new world,

It ended on a Wednesday night
when her boyfriend placed
a ring on their coffee table.
Later, she told me she cried
when she first saw it, went
into the bathroom and cried
some more, then said yes
after he came home from
walking her dogs. Maybe
he would be as stunned
and shaken by her answer
as I was, if he ever found
out how she spent that day,
her hands pressed against
the wall by my bed, legs
wrapped around my mouth,
biting back her moans
and screams, trying not
to show how good she felt.

A BETTER MAN

You know enough
not to stare,
but can't resist
picking your eyes
up off your book
when you turn
a page to watch
two guys snuggling,
whispering in the corner
seat of the F train
as if they're the first
two people to discover
love or lust. You know
how hard it can be
to find someone
to lift your loneliness,
how you should bless
and celebrate their miracle,
maybe even hope
it could happen to you
again someday. Instead,
you slow down, stare
at them like a car wreck
burning in the highway's
right lane, sirens blaring,
red lights flaring. Sorry,
you had always hoped
you'd be a better man.

1997

When you find a letter mixed in with tax returns and medical bills
from a woman you were much more into than she was ever into you,
you can't help thinking about your first night at her place and Dust
Bunnies by Bettie Serveert, an Indie band from Amsterdam, playing
on the stereo. The lead singer looked like a down home Blondie,
sounded like Lucinda and their songs still grace your mixed CDs.
You remember hummus, flaky pita bread, pickles, olives, sliced
cheese and making out on the couch. When Nancy stood up, turned
around and lifted her shirt while mildly criticizing herself for falling
in line, joining the latest fad but explaining she did design it herself,
she asked if you liked the slinky snakey shape emerging from beneath
her left shoulder blade, winding down past her hip, teasing the crack
of her ass. Knowing you would have loved her with or without it
undressed, you dropped down to your knees, sang hallelujah. Amen.

Circling a Village Voice personal ad, dialing numbers and trying
to locate your late night Barry White voice and making that first date
to meet outside The Bottom Line, her legs longer than advertised.
You listened to five folkies you would never hear of again in a Friday
night showcase, before strolling down Lower East Side streets where
she leaned in, tried to place a quick kiss on your lips in mid-stride
as you flinched away, surprised. You still wish you had slid your hands
down her sides, held her hips and guided her to the nearest tenement
to press her against the bricks for an urgent, make-out session
that lasted until sun rise while passersby slowed down to watch,
wishing they were you. And there's that one kick ass poem you wrote
about Nancy and her white fuzzy, just bought, Betsey Johnson top
that hung below her waist to brush her dark bush as she runwayed
across the bedroom floor, street light spilling through torn shades.

Only six months long, there wasn't a whole lot to you and Nancy:
Dion at Tramps singing Ruby Baby, her thinking it was a Steely Dan
cut, putting down her glass and clapping along as you sang Lovers
Who Wander too loud. Mentioning an early morning meeting, putting
the children's science mag she edited to bed, she bicycled east
while you headed to the subway, dick in hand. After spending a week
upstate with her family, she called the Saturday she returned, talked

66

about who knows what, your cock pressing against your fly. Somehow you never said why not catch a cab, come over, hang out, you'll order Spanish, Chinese, Mexican and she never said anything about wanting to come by, finally see your place. The night she ended it, she offered you a goodbye gift. If you wrote you left her something to remember, to miss, would anyone guess that you couldn't get it up, just kissed her neck instead, the double-lock latching tight as your shell tops hit the staircase?

ENDINGS

When you wake up with your first
throbbing hard-on since your kidney
transplant two Julys ago, you can't help
backtracking through the remnants
of last night's dreams to find Suzanne,
her playful teasing, soft brown eyes
that showed surprise, dismay and said
please so easily those three years she'd sneak
away from her long-time-live-in-boyfriend
to spend one or two early evenings a week
in your bed and how it filled your life
with sweet electricity. That was twenty
years ago and now she's turning forty,
the age you were when it all started
with her first managerial position,
mentoring sessions over Mexican lunches,
her trail of emails, a hushed phone
call, a walk in Brooklyn snowfall, boots
left at the door, a rushed early morning
goodbye and a return the next night.

Now you could think of Li-Young Lee,
his poem about seven different endings
and trying to give a name for that elastic
connection that bends and binds lovers
together so everyone knows what's going
on between them, or that Hoagland poem
where if you call something love, more
and more questions that grow harder
and harder to answer reach the surface
until you find your own unhappy ending.
You linked your pinkies, pulled and swore
on a god only one of you believed in
that it was real love. She'd say abracadabra,
wish Bill would disappear and you still
wish you had the chance to be together

Or you could go online and find out about
the school for autistic kids she founded
outside of Austin, her three beautiful
daughters and her wonderful husband,
the many furry, four legged family
members that fill their house. You nod,
know that's what she said she always
wanted. You doubt she ever thinks
about you since she could pretend
Bill didn't exist at will. Watching
her eager intern sliding across the floor
to reach the wild five year old, banging
his head on the floor, you wonder
if she goes back to when you first met
and sees herself, the way he quiets him
with sing song phrases until the kid
quits flailing his arms, kicking fiercely
and takes two slow breaths, lies still.

Maybe as she lingers in the parking lot,
plays with her car keys as the intern,
let's call him Ryan, talks about his toughest
and favorite kids, she looks at herself
and finds hints of the way you leaned in,
listened to her back then and she remembers
hours talking about Neko Case's new record,
Lost In Translation, driving to the batting
cages and grabbing the best slice of pizza
in Brooklyn. Does she ever close her eyes,
imagine that scruffy young guy, his untucked
flannel shirt, when she's lying in bed
letting the day unwind? When her husband
begins to knead her shoulders, trace
the bony bumps in the back of her neck
with his fingertips, does she feel
your ringless fingers wrap around
her shoulders, cup her breasts, pull
her closer before she buries her head
deeper into the pillows and tells Bill,
not tonight, sorry, it was a long day?

LAST LOVE POEM

It was only a few days,
maybe a week, before
I was able to tuck my fists
back into my pockets,
before my steps once again
found their easy, not quite,
graceful rhythm when walking
past the deserted schoolyard
where I was mugged on my way
to work. My head finally
stopped swiveling side to side
any time some brown skinned kid
hurried across the street
and the cold steel feel
of the gun pressed against
my neck disappeared beneath
summer's sweat and I felt
safe, free to come and go
from early morning light
through darkening nights.

It took months of riding
the F train, before the smoke
and dust settled, the hushed
church-like quiet lifted and all
the sad, heavy eyes quit
drifting out the windows
to silently stare at the shadows
of the two towers still hovering
in the air. Everyone eventually
went back to scrambling
for the last vacant seat, splashes
of static and bone throbbing bass
started leaking once again
from turned up headphones
and the homeless hordes
no longer held their breath

and stopped begging
for spare change until
the train burrowed back
under the ground. Old,
hunched over, Asian men
began selling batteries, two
for a dollar, once more. Eyes
scanned newspapers for trending
stocks and basketball standings
once again. Not one stray tear
traced down anyone's cheek.

But even after thirty years,
I still sometimes find myself
reaching across the mattress
expecting to bring you closer
first thing in the morning.
Whenever the phone rings
interrupting my chronic daydreams,
I am always disappointed
it's never your sultry, sleepy voice
on the line chanting my name.
And yes I am often tempted
to see if I'm the kind of writer
who can find the right words
to ask, no beg, you to leave
your husband and come back
to where you always belonged
or simply sneak off for a few
hours so I can take your hand,
cross teeming city streets
and unlock my apartment door,
rest your head in my lap.
I want to close my eyes, listen
to you fill in every missing, lost
moment and dream of leaning over,
finding your lips and kissing
the one woman I never stopped
loving, one last time before I die.

PLAYING POET ON A SATURDAY IN DUMBO

Thirty years ago, I'd meet Dave
my friend from work down here,
run full court before white people
discovered this part of Brooklyn
Back then, he lived for free
in a shut-down church as part
of some residency working
with the homeless, a half block
from the projects. Mugged twice,
he signed up for martial arts,
carried a knife and got shot
in the York Street subway tunnel
when he wouldn't give up
his wallet a third time.

Today, it's poets meeting
at a bar with smiles, half hugs.
When we start to talk about
writing, the constant rejection,
teaching gigs, poets we know
in common, current projects,
the difference between creative
non-fiction and narrative poetry,
and does any of it really matter
since no one reads anymore
anyway, it's easy to forget
that years ago, we all found
words on pages that made
us feel a little less alone, opened
our eyes to different, deeper
ways of seeing and feeling
with a kind of music that sings
in our skin and started to write.

I keep checking on the Yankees-
Indians game, imagine the bartender
naked every time she leans over.

More poets arrive and we're happy.
Especially me, because I believe
this means we will eat soon.
Busy with my three tacos
while everyone keeps talking,
I think about my real job, Thursday's
emergency meeting, impending
layoffs, Larry's advancing dementia
and now fewer staff to care for him.

A short walk to our evening reading
at Berl's, an all poetry book store.
I browse shelves, so many poets,
like me, no one's ever heard of.
I sit at the end of the back row,
five readers will come and go.
One practices alphabet gymnastics
and the sound clusters tumble, twirl
over my head. The second reads
each poem, tears the pages out.
They float to the floor like dying
butterflies. The next one rips
his pages, slowly eats them
making faces as he chews.
People laugh, not me. I hope
he chokes. Someone cracks,
anyone know the Heimlich Maneuver.
I do, but I'm not getting up.

Introduced, I read four pieces
about the woman I loved most,
her abortion, how that time
still haunts me; the nurse
at dialysis, her son's memorial
day, the way we connected
over Monk's Bemsha Swings;
a playful, unlikely affair; Jesse,
my sort of stepson, severely
autistic, and the first time

he hugged me, saying goodbye
at the airport, the nearly
ten seconds he held me. Happy
with how my poems felt leaving
my mouth and filling the air
despite a few coughs, my tongue
stumbling over some syllables,
I hardly hear the next reader.

I subway home with headphones
playing, but Monday intrudes
on the walk to my apartment,
when I'll talk to three people,
one after another, saying
I have bad news, apologizing,
thanking them for their years
of service as my voice breaks,
the words thudding to the floor
with a kind of force I hope
all my poems somehow find.

TRANSPLANT

Everyone tells me
I'm a lucky man,
blessed and fortunate
to have four willing donors.
And I know they're right,
people wither away
waiting for kidneys
on endless lists
with no guarantees.
I've talked to doctors,
did extensive research
and came away convinced
it's a highly successful
procedure. Everyone's
encouraging, assuring me
it's not nearly as bad
as last year's open heart
surgery and my two friends
with transplants are both
alive and living normal lives.
And yes, I am so sick
of dialysis, three times
a week for three and a half
hours a session with its sudden
blood pressure drops
and crippling cramps
that leave me hobbling
around like a slow motion
half dazed zombie who only
wants to sleep my life away
that I'd do almost anything.

My youngest brother proved
a perfect match. We're looking
at July when his work slows down
and his wife's school breaks
for summer so she can watch

75

their kids while he recovers.
There's no way to thank him
and yes, I can hardly wait.
Except my mind keeps
filling up with thoughts
of something going wrong,
something bad happening
to him during the operation,
and then who will tell me
what to say to his wife,
to his kids, Daniel and Lexie.

MEMORY

I am starting to forget things. Especially names.
The slick speedy short stop who hit clean-up
for our championship softball team? The first
girl I kissed in spin the bottle, tall and blonde
with freckles on the bridge of her nose bending
to meet my lips? The doctor who performed
my open heart surgery? The new executive
director who signs my checks? In the middle
of a conversation about something essential:
life, death, black and white, sports or music
there's this word or phrase simmering
somewhere inside my mind that summarizes,
encapsulates, wins any argument and damn
it never finds my tongue as the conversation
rolls on without me. Last night, I saw Dylan
at The Beacon Theater and in the third verse
of Tangled Up In Blue, a song that breaks
my heart every time, I had to stop singing
along because I had lost the words, somehow
I couldn't remember something I knew I'd never
forget. Out of nowhere, these names, words,
faces will reappear, show up without any fanfare
and for a moment they settle in my thoughts
and are all mine again, but then I realize how
easily I can lose so much and it terrifies me, how
fragile my mind, my world, can turn out to be.

But I have never forgotten my great grandmother,
that black shawled, gnarled up old lady everyone
whispered about with words like crazy and senile,
how she'd sit at the table and grumble in Italian
about my born with polio Uncle Dom running around
gambling and chasing women. She'd suddenly,
periodically scream where's Mgoots as he sat back
in his puffed up leather lounge chair, his crutches
and braces stationed by his side, trying to watch
wrestling on the tiny black and white screen.

The way we sat down for a dinner of countless
courses and streams of piss puddled around
her feet. We kept eating as Aunt Rosie or Josie
reached for the mop like nothing happened
and how we were all forced to kiss, hug
everyone goodbye as she clung to my baby
brother, screaming that my mom was stealing
her bambino as my mom lifted, grabbed John
and passed him to my father like a steaming ravioli.

GRANDPA'S HANDS

Were soft pillows
covered with thick tough
skin   they lifted me over
turnstiles   up ramps

for first glimpses of Campy,
Pee Wee, Jackie   put
shiny dimes in open palms
dared me to snatch them

away   snuck cupped Camels
on crowded buses   shuffled,
cut, dealt hours of blackjack
for pennies   they rubbed

my new summer crew
cut   bribed me with crisp
dollar bills when we missed
Mass to watch slow-pitch

softball   they faked left jabs,
right hooks, then snuck upper
cuts beneath my peek-a-boo
stance   held the chain link fence

tight   waved goodbye
while our rented Ryder truck
backed out the driveway
and left for Long Island in '67

SHAGGING FLIES

The last hour of light
slips behind the backstop.
My father stands at home plate.
I trot to the outfield,
stand with my legs spread
shoulder length apart.
Bent slightly at the waist,
I place my hands on my knees,
lean my weight forward
and wait for him to toss
the ball up, swing the bat.
Crack. The sound sings
in my skin. I take
that first cross-over
step, get my legs
in gear, track the ball
down. I catch it,
cradle it in the web,
peg it back on one hop.
Crack. The Mick sprints
to the base of the monuments,
makes a back hand stab,
pulls up with his slight limp.
Crack. Crack. Yaz turns
his back to the plate,
watches the line drive
dent the Green Monster.
He whirls, unfurls
a perfect strike,
catches the runner
sliding into second.
Crack. Crack. Mary Ellen's
seventh grade mouth
drifts down from heaven,
kisses my lips, slow
dances with my tongue.
Crack. Crack. Crack. I catch

my breath, lick sweat
off my upper lip. Crack.
Crack. Clemente charges
a hard hit single,
picks it up thigh high,
fires it home on a fly.
Crack. Aaron lopes back
to the warning track,
feels for the fence,
braces himself, leaps
and snatches the ball
out of a fan's hands.
Crack. A shooting star
falls, lands in my mitt.
I fling it back with all
my might, watch it grow
wings, fly and splash
the twilight with blazing
bright lights. Crack. Willie
glides after a broken bat
blooper, loses his hat
to Candlestick winds,
catches the ball in his basket
and races my father home.

AUTISTIC JOY

I love telling friends about the times I forget
to lock the closets that help keep Jesse safe
so he can live in this apartment on his own
and I catch him pouring a bottle of dishwasher
detergent into the sink or shredding a pack
of multi colored post-its as he sits at the kitchen
counter, flips them into the air like confetti.
He freezes, tries not to look at me and places
his hand over his mouth as this boundless
sound spills out, his eyes bubbly blue champagne,
while his body shakes in shivers of happiness.
His mom calls it the best laugh and it's one
of the few things we still agree on. I try to look
stern as I count seconds until his laughter slows
down and I move closer, poke his soft ticklish
spots to stretch this moment. I tell myself
next visit I'll buy the biggest bottle of soda,
place it on the table where he can find it
as I shut the bathroom door behind me.

November, and the ground is feathered white,
the wind swirls a light sprinkling. We'll start
our weekend with a City Bus trip to Starbucks.
He looks at his lap top, tells me the exact time
and I say, *let's get dressed.* He says, *no socks.*
I say, *yes socks.* He says, *short sleeves.* I say,
long sleeves, it's freezing out there. He says,
light jacket. I say, *heavy coat. Red jacket.*
Green coat. Back and forth, four more times
until I say *hurry we'll miss the bus.* He streaks
to his room while I grab my coat, tug my hat
over my ears and toss him the keys to lock
the door as I try to zip my coat. Halfway down
the hall, he starts cracking up, falling over

himself, laughing. I look at him. He's wearing
the green coat and zipping the red jacket
over it. I'm laughing hard, reaching for a hug.
Jesse pulls his head back, stares into my eyes
to make sure I know he did this all for me.

SONGS AND ILLUMINATIONS

Flying home from visiting Jesse,
you're strapped in for the hour flight.
A young woman, all flush and out
of breath, stops at your row, apologizes
with her eyes for making you get up.
You fumble with the seat belt, struggle
with your cane like a creaky invalid
or a shy schoolboy as you rise
to let her slide by. Thirty years ago
when you were young and a whole man,
she'd still be too cool and pretty for you.
If you tried to start a conversation now,
she'd turn your way, nod, be polite
and sweet, maybe pat you on the wrist
as if you were harmless. But the scent
of her hair fills you up and her tight
ass brushes your crotch and you hope
for the start of a hard-on as you try
to recall the last time you were this close
to someone so beautifully alive. You both
fit headphones on. Music, the one thing
that hasn't abandoned you. You daydream
while flying over some wooded expanse
that the same song is whispering secrets
into both of your ears while you both
sing along as it leads you home.

For now, Van Morrison's playing
Tupelo Honey and already you miss
Jesse, the autistic boy you took as your own
when you lived with his mom. You love
the way he lives in his own apartment,
staff supervising him twelve hours a day,
cameras and locks keeping him safe
overnight. You love how he smiles
as soon as he sees you, rides city
buses to eat at his favorite places,

84

how he talks more and more after
years of silence, how his patience
has lengthened, tolerance for change
grown. You wish you lived closer,
had more say in his life. Maybe
they'd listen when you complain
how staff make him quiet down,
lower his happily humming voice
even in his own home, or force him
to march with the group on this soft
spring day as he walks to the water
fountain for a short break, the way
he vaults in the air, stomps his two
feet on the ground, folds into a fist
and begins to bite his wrist. Angry
and frustrated, you shake your head,
wish he'd bite his workers instead.

Across the grassy field teenagers
are running full court, nobody playing
defense, too much show boating,
one on one play. You picture
yourself bringing the ball up court,
finding the tall black guy down low
for an easy basket. Over by the stream
a blue jeaned beauty is walking a big
brown dog as you lip-synch words
you could say to her while staff waits
the three minutes for Jesse to collect
himself, take ten deep breaths and hold
his hands in prayer to show he's ready
for work. You look at him, wonder
if he knows all the things your lives
are missing on this breezy April day.

Before leaving, you agreed you'd be back
in June for dinner at Texas Roadhouse.
That evening, June 14th, you got tickets
for Brian Wilson, your musical god,

who has lived longer than anyone
expected. He's playing *Pet Sounds*
and you wish Jesse could tolerate
crowds and flashing lights to sit
next to you, get to his feet, clap
along to the brightly lit *Wouldn't
It Be Nice* with its infectious melody
and climbing harmonies, close
his eyes, let his spirit fill
as Brian hits most of the notes
of the holy *God Only Knows.*
Instead, you'll ask Jesse's mom
who stopped loving you years ago
to the show. After, with *Love
and Mercy* still lingering
in your ears, she'll drop you off
at Jesse's apartment and you'll check
that he's sleeping, that everything's
intact, nothing's been poured
on the floor, no clothes torn.
You'll unfold the couch, make
your bed and hopefully sleep
until Jesse wakes you for a 7:30 bus.

Breuger's Bagels. He'll order a plain bagel
with peanut butter from the counter girl
who won't understand him the first time.
You'll ask him to say it again, slower, clearer.
He'll find a blue drink from the giant
glassy refrigerator and slide into a booth
as you wait for a steamy hot chocolate.
He'll watch you drink the last sip, crush
the cup, drop it into the trash. Finished,
you'll walk two blocks to the bus stop.
Jesse will keep looking back. Slowing
down, he'll let you catch up, wrap
your arm around his shoulder
as he never stops humming
his beautiful, unnamable song.

ALMOST SUMMER ON THE B61 TO RED HOOK

You know summer's nearly
here when you climb
on the bus and the blasting
air conditioner gives you
instant goose bumps. You find
a seat. Three Puerto Rican
high school angels own
the back row, one more
beautiful and streetier, sexier
than the other, in their torn
cut-offs and clingy tees. Old
enough to be instantly dismissed
you try not to stare. It's impossible.
One's tapping her cell phone,
fingernails perfectly shaped
and indigo blue, clicking beats
to sounds sliding down her spine.
She stares at endless texts, leans
back, laughs. She reaches it over.
The one staring at a mirror,
moving it up, down, slanting it
to discover the perfect angle
is busy brushing, sculpting,
fine tuning her lethal eye brows
as if life depended on it, glances
over, nods and lets a sly smile
linger across those luscious lips.
If you were thirty years younger,
the third is the one you'd want
most. Sort of sleepy looking,
slightly tousled, she stares out
the window, sees everything
or nothing at all, pays no mind
to what the other two are doing.
Deeper eyes, darker hair, she gets

up, walks to the door and when
she steps into the street
you can tell by her slow easy
rhythm she's starting to realize
that guys believe she holds
all the keys to the kingdom
and is beginning to imagine
what she will do with them.

CRYING

It's an early Monday morning
and I'm leaning against the door
of the E train, scanning the faces
of other riders. My eyes stumble
on a well dressed black man sitting
across the car, crying quietly,
streaks making their way down
his face, shoulders starting to stutter
until he bends over, tries to cover
his face with his dark brown fedora.

I look around, half the passengers
are lost to their iPhones, the others
are either looking away defiantly,
or like me, trying to believe their eyes,
feeling uncomfortable, hoping someone
would get up, do something. Maybe
the Spanish grandmother reading
her Bible. She can offer a quote, fill him
with spirit and hope, maybe put an arm
around him, pull him close. A little girl
asks her mom *why is that man crying*
as the train pulls into Queensboro Plaza.
I dash across the platform to catch
my transfer, miss the answer.

All day that man's tears stay with me,
make me recall how my ex once cried
for who knows why by the turnstile
at the West Fourth Street station,
how easily, how often she would start
to cry over something I did or didn't do,
her frustration at the way the world
never fell into place, her endless worry
over what will happen to her autistic son
when she lies down and dies, exhausted.
I remember how I loved to hold her,
the times I helped her and the time
I tried not to cry when she decided
she was better off, happier, without me.

89

PART OF THE JOB

When the new worker
forgot to give the new resident
his favorite coffee mug
Monday morning, he called her
a dumb nigger. She left me a note
saying she needed to see me
at my earliest convenience.
Tuesday, she sat in my office,
angry and teary eyed. I explained
that Frankie doesn't know
what he's saying, doesn't
know what the word signifies.
That's why he lives here,
that's why we have jobs.
He says it to see the look
on your face change, show
himself he has some power,
some control in his own life.
I said I could only imagine
how she must feel, told her
I was sorry, but it's always
best to keep a blank face,
an even voice. It's never easy
but you can't take anything
personal, it's part of the job.

I told her about the time
I didn't tie Larry's sneakers
the exact way he likes
and he kicked me in the chest
with both feet and knocked me
flat on my back, how badly
I wanted to jump up, grab
his bald head, knee him
in the nuts, but didn't.
I didn't say anything
about putting my fist

through the bulletin board,
papers flying, sliding across
the floor. I said I asked him
to calm down, waited a half
minute while I lifted my shirt,
traced the red mark gingerly,
then leaned over, tried to tie
his laces the right damn way.

NAMES IN MY HEAD

Before we sit down at the table
for Monday's shift meeting,
the guy whose name everybody
gave up pronouncing and started
calling Joko says he had a rough
weekend. His sister died. I say damn,
I'm sorry, hope he doesn't want to talk
about it. We've worked together
nearly a dozen years. I'm the boss,
he's a direct care worker and unlike
most of the people in the place,
we've never really connected.
I struggle with his African accent,
long sentences he blurts out, loud
and too fast, how his face crinkles
into a question mark whenever
I crack a joke, try to be ironic. We both
love the guys who live at the group
home and trust each other to carry
more than our share of the load.
Usually, we talk about overtime,
double shifts, lifting Larry out
of his bed, wheeling him down
to the corner bodega for ice cream,
driving Lee to his weekly massage.

Today, Joko talks slowly, softly,
explains he hadn't seen his sister
in eight years. She lived in England,
died on a list waiting for a kidney.
He knows all about my disease,
saw what it did to me. I think
about Jaime, my youngest brother
offering to be a donor, his kidney
a perfect match, giving me back
my old, normal life. I don't mention
Michael, Elisa, Erica, all willing to be,

if needed, back up donors. Afraid
to ask, I wonder if Joko was tested.
I don't want to put him on the spot
and I know I'd think less of him
if he gave the wrong answer. Instead,
I name names in my head, a long list
of friends who would have let me die.

LARRY

Because we've taken such good care of him,
Larry's lived long enough to start showing signs
of dementia. Sometimes, it can be difficult to tell
the difference between possible signs and his quirky,
comical mannerisms. Yes, he had already stopped
pirouetting like a clumsy teddy bear every ten steps
or so, stopped reaching down to pull up his socks.
In fact, he hasn't worn socks in fifteen years.
Even yesterday, with wind blown snow
steadily swirling, I couldn't change his mind
before we walked to the corner bodega
and his buddy behind the counter gave him
his usual: coffee, black, two sugars. These days
he eats with his fingers more than his fork
and the other night when I slid the cover
off his straw, handed it to him, he tried
to suck up a rippled potato chip. He dropped
the straw, spread his arms wide in a *what
the fuck* gesture until I rubbed his neck,
pushed his cup closer. Sometimes, on the way
to his bedroom, he turns left instead, walks
downstairs, spends a half hour shooting
on our basement hoop. Recently, he's hit
himself, a quick jab to the jaw a few times,
but he's done stuff like that before. Years ago
he smashed his arm through the front window.
A flood of blood poured out and his bicep
looked like chopped meat. We spent the night
in the ER while he drank three Diet Cokes,
made faces, sounds and hand signals that cracked
the orderlies up. We've held weekly meetings
with our nurse, social worker, psychologist;
constructed baseline charts, set up medical
appointments, talked about what to expect,
how bad things might get, possible alternate

placement options. But he still recognizes
everyone, asks for Kevin to work every night,
slides his hand over his smooth dome indicating
he wants a shave, greets me with a sideways
lingering hug, still moves into me when I palm
his head like a Nerf basketball and every evening
when my shift ends, he walks me to the door,
opens it and says *comin' tomorrow* at least twice.
Last night, he kept walking: through the doorway,
down the stoop, past the gate in his slow, side to side
Charlie Chaplin shuffle, all the way out to the curb.
I shadowed him, hugged him from behind, pressed
my face to his cheek, whispered something soft,
something silly, and helped him grab the handrail,
walk inside while I told him he wasn't going anywhere.

JOHN AND THE TEENAGE COUPLE

While everyone at the group home
races through dinner in fifteen minutes
or less, perhaps unable to forget
their years spent in Willowbrook,
the other patients who snatched
the food off their plates, John
takes hold of the serving dish
and fills his plate carefully, neatly
separating meat from vegetables,
mashed potatoes pushed as far away
as possible. He whispers to ten
with each bite, lets the food
tumble past his Adam's Apple,
stabs another forkful, pauses
on the way to his mouth, surveys
the room for signs of danger before
bringing the food past his lips.

At neighborhood stores, he stands
in front of the floor-to-ceiling,
refrigerated glass case or stocked
shelves, rubbing his hands, mulling
over this life and death decision
until he reaches down, grabs a pack
of Yankee Doodles. He walks
to the counter glowing. *Hello,*
my name's John, what's your name.
The guy behind the cash register,
head burrowed in his cell phone
grunts, *dollar fifty.* John digs
his wallet out of his pocket,
holds it close to his chest, picks
a wrinkly bill from its sleeve. One
by one, he places pennies and dimes
on the counter, counting the amount
out loud as a teenage, hand-in-hand
couple saunters through the door.

The girl in tight ripped jeans, nipples
pressing against her cut off tee, lingers
up front, running her fingernails
across breath mints and gum, trying
to make eye contact with the guy
behind the counter as her boyfriend
roams the aisles stuffing his pockets,
sliding a pack of cold cuts under
his shirt, inside his waistband.
I watch John slow down even more
while the folks waiting in line turn
to me. But I know John wants to do this
on his own. He doesn't like anyone
touching his money and he's hoping
the cashier will discover he's mentally
challenged, find a bit of pity and decide
he deserves free Friday night cup cakes.

WHAT WORK REALLY IS

Friends ask why stay? You turn
sixty-five in June, live in a rent
controlled apartment, can afford
to retire. It's an hour and a half
bus and subway commute each
way between Queens and Red Hook.
The new executive director looks
like Michelle Obama, acts like
Donald Trump. Long time
workers have been forced
to leave, support staff laid off,
care compromised. You'll miss,
no, mourn, this place, the people
who work, who live here, taken
from Willowbrook as teens,
integrated into the community.
Your friends say their lives
have been better because
you wound up here. You know
all they've meant to your life.
Though you never believed
anything was meant to be,
you recognize how unlikely
it was you found your way
here, stayed forty years, helped
shape this home into something
you consider sacred. You tell
friends, you don't want to stay
home, write. You've always
found time for that and nobody
is dying, waiting for anyone's poetry.
You're worried, afraid loneliness
could deepen, boredom escalate.

Tamara yells from down the hall.
She needs help getting Larry
to the bathroom. *One, two, three.*

Up. Take a breath. *Steady?* Now,
help him shuffle to the toilet.
You latch his hands around
the towel rack, grab hold
under his arms. She bends,
pulls, and yanks his pants
all the way down when Larry
clearly says '*I got it.*' Tamara,
you, look at each other. His first
words since advanced dementia.
You both crack up, land high fives
as she tears his under-alls off, starts
to wash his pale, shrunken ass.

GENTRIFICATION

Warren Residence, 1979-2016

The first time you subwayed to the group home was back in '79.
You got off one F stop too late, ran down Smith. Running out
of breath, you took the right on Warren. Italian restaurants
and butcher shops with Mafia tough guys sprawled out front
had turned into Puerto Rican rice and beans spots with Virgin
Marys standing in the windows, arms opened wide, blessing
the tan card table where grandfathers played dominoes. Black
corner boys lifted cigarettes to their lips in cupped hands,
looked you up and down as you trotted toward the projects.
Halfway down the block, the group home, your first job.
All incoming staff sat in rows of folding chairs as psychologists
and nuns spoke about the six boys coming from institutions
at the end of the month, their low functioning levels, problematic
behaviors, self injurious ways, their inability to hold a conversation
or follow simple directions. You heard all about the biters, self
abusers, runners you could never leave alone, the one who ripped
his clothes and threw his shoes, one who picked his skin, chewed
the scabs for hours, one who tried to gouge out his own eyes,
the deaf one, three with seizures, the one who banged his head,
the autistic kid who never looked anyone in the eye, shrieked all day.

Break time, you sat on the stoop alone, the only white person left
in the world, feeling more Caucasian than ever. Scanning burnt out,
abandoned buildings, rusted cars with smashed windows, you thought
of your father working two jobs he hated to move your family out
of this kind of neighborhood to Long Island lawns. Through the window,
the Spanish women spoke their rat-a-tat machine gun language probably
about the blanco, your tattered jeans, down to the ass hippie hair. Black
guys grasped hands in secret handshakes as if they played schoolyard
basketball for years together, knew each other's moms, sisters by face,
by name. You sat there wondering how to resign gracefully, sprint
back to where you belonged: Kew Gardens, brick houses, wide quiet
streets, white people. But you needed a job. The girl you loved

and just moved in with was expecting half the rent and this looked
like your best choice. You worried about riding the F train at night,
how many times you'd get mugged, whether you'd ever get home alive.

You stayed and slowly started to feel like you sort of fit in, like everybody
else, in this not for profit Catholic residence. You fell for the kids instantly.
Robert, shaky on his feet and always smiling, thanking you for everything;
Larry, asking for you on your days off, waiting for you to carry him off
his school bus, wrapped in a bath towel because he tore all his clothes
again, his Fruit of the Looms knotted around his balls; sitting on the couch
waiting for the night shift to take your place, talking basketball, jazz;
plates of collard greens, mondongo, black eyed peas, empanadas, pig's
feet placed in front of you, eating every bite, asking for more, every time.
Please. Thank you. You took your turn taking the toughest kids, showering
them without gagging any time they shitted or bloodied themselves; how
Jose introduced you to all his friends saying you were alright for being
white an all; the way Larry holds your hand and walks you to the door
and says tomorrow every night, that morning you CPR'd Jimmy
and he still died; John Burns choking on a sticky bun at day program,
dying; head bowed at family funerals, the pews shaking and moaning
with the lifting choir; that backyard barbecue when Liz soaked you
with the hose in a pagan baptism, yelling stop being so damn quiet
boy or you'd have to find yourself some other sweet black mama.

35 years and two muggings later, Boerum Hill has turned into another
too cool for its own good Brooklyn neighborhood. Bearded white guys
with shoulder bags saunter down the street, young white women walk
their perfectly groomed dogs or stand on stoops, smoke and constantly
scroll iPhones, black women pack white babies into strollers built
like tanks and roll over streets like invading armies. Bars, restaurants
with sidewalk tables and bright blue umbrellas, open, close weekly.
Cookie, Jimmy Boy, Liz, Grandma, Gladys, too long dead. Michelle,
lost to the pipe, Jose, AIDS. Ernesto, Robert the Penis, Grot, Emilio,
Yusef, Shawn, White Shawn, JJ, Jasmine, Jamilia you can call her J
with her cut off tees and deep neighborhood eyes, Lois and her fine
light skin daughter gone to higher paying jobs. Coney Island Jack
and should have been gay Greg, doctors and professors in North

Carolina, Maryland. Nancy, Mean Jean, Regina retired. Shameka, lazy ass Sylvia, Charles the African, fired. Blaze, Bones own big houses down near Atlanta. Jaime Luis living on disability in P.R. Joko, Tamara, Tamika, Kevin, Gwen, Chris, Devon, Moses, Reesy, you, still working your asses off. The landlord sold the building last month for over three and a half million. Date to vacate, January 31st. How do you say goodbye, find another place where six mentally challenged low functioning men belong? Genuflect. Cross yourself and bow your head. Larry Larry Larry, Now and at the hour. Amen.

SOME LONG AGO SUMMER

Once upon a time I slept with a woman
who worked a few months at the group
home I run, but only after I fired her
for a no call no show weekend that left
the shifts severely understaffed. Next day,
we ran into each other on the subway,
rode through Manhattan together,
hugged goodbye. Four days later,
Denise waited for me outside work, went
all the way home with me. After fucking
the night away, we went to the diner
for breakfast. Grits for her, home fries
for me. We ended up at the schoolyard.
She took me down low, bumped me
with her lovely ass, while I tried
to ignore my hard-on. I kept the score
close, but always won. She was younger,
I was older. I had money, she had none.
I was lighter, she was darker. She was
beautiful, I was not. We never could agree
on a radio station. We both liked Al Green,
but never the same songs. She loved
the back to back black shows on NBC
Thursday nights, I preferred Law
and Order. She never read my poetry.
I felt her rap rhymes silly and forced.
She liked things rough and hard, I liked
to watch my cum slide slowly down
her dark inner thighs. I didn't know
if she was hoping to get her job back,
looking for some kind of love or a few
weekends of outside the neighborhood
fun. I wasn't doing any thinking at all.
Just last week, she was standing in line
at the corner bodega. Coffee for her,

Snapple for me. She still looked good.
Me, worse than before. Once, she said,
she saw me walking by in some long ago
summer as she sat in a shady park rocking
her baby for an afternoon nap. She said
I never looked her way, but she knows
if I did I would have stopped, leaned
down for a soft quick kiss and told her
that her daughter was as beautiful
as she is. I smiled, knew she was right.

DETROIT

When you step up to the ticket window,
the sweet smiling sexy twenty year old
hands you your ticket and change, says
she likes your shirt, a deep purple tee
with a print of an Indian chief on horseback,
his war-bonneted head raised high, leaning
back triumphantly, arms spread wide
taking the whole world in and celebrating
the Beach Boys, fifty years of harmony.
You stand there, wonder how weird
it would be to dub her a mixed CD
of Brian's little known gems. You'd joke,
explain that you are part of an official
musical mission and all women as beautiful
as she should have a little holiness sprinkled
in with her *fun fun fun*. As you walk in,
she tells you their songs never grow old,
unlike you, who is trying not to imagine
her undressing, your hands lightly cupping
the curve of her ass. It's a mid week matinee
and the theater is nearly empty. You could sit
in the back row, jerk off if you wanted to,
but the movie is *Detroit* and the smooth,
shiny Motown grooves of the Temptations,
Martha and her Vandellas, Marvin, Tammi,
fill in every background lull and build up
tension when *A Little Bit Of Soul* slips in,
brings you back to Queens, stickball in the street,
throw it up and hit a Spaldeen two sewers long
while Eddie Berne's band rehearsed, singing
You gotta make like you wanna kneel and pray
And then a little bit of soul will come your way
over and over in his garage for Friday night's
St Ann's dance. Jackie, the third best player
in the neighborhood is starting to sprout tits.
She'd probably laugh, make a face or punch
you in the shoulder if you asked her to dance

or mentioned anything about her sister sitting
on her porch, strapped to a wheelchair,
spastically waving her arms and moaning
the day away. At thirteen, you didn't know
anyone black. Everyone was Irish or Italian
or Jewish. A Chinese guy owned the laundry.
Sometimes you'd stand in the doorway,
make deep loud guttural sounds until
he came out shaking his fists and yelling
gibberish as you ran down the block, out
of breath, and laughing. Back on the screen,
Detroit is burning. The cops closed down
an all black after hours spot, piled everyone
into vans as a simmering crowd gathered.
The colored folks went crazy and the police
went crazier and everyone knows the cops
will get away with everything in the end.

DOWN BY AN OLD MILL WHERE A BIG PART OF YOUR HEART LIVES

The bus driver motions you
to climb on when you read
the address of your step son's
apartment. *Get off at the mill.*
Then, a few blocks down the road.
You've lived your whole life
in NYC, imagine that mills look
like factories in Springsteen songs.
You picture a big building,
red brick or gray sheet rock.
Maybe a little town built itself
around it. A whistle blows.
Bunches of hunched over men,
hands in pockets, or one arm
hanging down, carrying a battered
lunch box, walk through some gate
in a misty dusk, sucking on cigarettes,
the dots of light pulsing from their lips.
Some turn left to one of two corner bars,
others veer right, head for dinner tables.
Almost, you can hear a faint harmonica,
a soft tone from The Big Man's sax.

You are neither going home or out
for a Friday night of beer, 8 ball,
and a bar band. No, it's a weekend
spent visiting Jesse. If you see
your long ago girl friend, you'll both
act cordial. When you try, you can still
recall things you loved about her,
although you know she would never
think of trying. But you and Jesse
have a gift. You can both stop time.
He's autistic and you love the kid,
who's now a man. The bus driver
announces, Blainefield Mill. You walk

to the door, nod thanks. No mill,
just a large building filled with offices,
clothing shops, an organic market,
a sleek restaurant overlooking
a waterfall fed by melting snow.

The fourth floor apartment door opens
and Jesse's support worker yells, *look
who's here.* Jesse says *Tony,* glances
at you sideways with a big smile. You ask
him what's new: He's living on his own
in this new beautiful apartment, three
spacious rooms, stained wooden floors,
glazed windows flooding the place
with sun, central air conditioning
and this bearded, doo-ragged worker
you never met who extends his hand,
says his name is Brandon. You own
a new kidney and unlike last time,
you're walking without a cane.
Jesse has added a few soft pounds
to his middle. You catch his eye, *say
what's going on, man, I've missed you*
and Jesse who habitually answers "good"
to most questions, surprises you by saying
not much and you laugh, realize he's right.
Nothing essential has changed. It's just you
and Jesse, moving closer for your brief hug.

AUTISTIC BASKETBALL

You are following Jesse
through a new-to-you part
of his neighborhood. You ask
if he knows where he's going,
how far, and he says *straight*.
You ask again, he points ahead.
You sat at the morning table
listing activities on the page
he titled Saturday September 15.
He chose basketball instead
of the Lake Champlain ferry.
He walks with his two hands
in front of him, holding the ball
like a mechanical waiter
balancing a tray. No dribbling
between his legs, behind his back,
no stutter stepping or head faking,
no flipping it back and forth
between you and him, no racing
across the court, a pass floating
in the air, catching you in stride
as you rise with the memory
of your first taste of schoolyard
grace and lay it softly against
the backboard so the ball settles
in the net's momentary embrace.

Basketball with Jesse means
taking turns for a certain number
of shots. You negotiate, he agrees
reluctantly to 10. You haven't touched
any kind of ball in 7 years: kidney
disease, open heart surgery, hernia
strangulation, dialysis, and finally
the kidney transplant. You run
out of breath trotting a half block
to catch your morning bus, cling

to a pole as it drives, afraid
you'll fall across the aisle
as it turns onto the service
road. You walk slowly, watch
where your feet land. You stand
at the foul line. Jesse's a step
and a half in front of you.
He shoots first with a stiff, over
the head, Jack Sikma-like release
that banks in. You're next, still
trying to imitate Earl The Pearl
of the long gone Baltimore Bullets.
He counts the shots down, only
smiles when he gets to shout
10 so he can go home, sit
at the table, cross basketball
off his list, move on to McKee's:
apple juice with ice, chicken
fingers, French fries, extra hot.
Jesse's 10 for 10, You're 1 for 10
with an air ball. He doesn't care.
You have to tell yourself not to.

WINDOWS

I don't remember all the details,
but I doubt the real estate agent
focused on the window light
in my apartment. One bedroom,
rent stabilized, good neighborhood,
a quick subway ride into the city
was what I wanted. Eating, I look
out the kitchen window and tree
branches nearly brush against it.
Occasionally, I watch a leaf let go.
Another window stares at bricks,
windows from other wings
of the building. Curtains, shades
always drawn, I've lost all hope
of ever seeing a naked woman
stroll by to help me remember
a younger, happier day or two.
The bedroom window overlooks
a one way street. Sometimes
a guy or girl walks down it,
always alone. When he or she
carries an umbrella I know
for sure it's raining. Mostly,
I keep my shades pulled down.

Winter and no baseball games
to watch, I listen to retired
players talk about last
or next season, predict
who will be traded where,
who deserves to be voted
into the Hall of Fame, who
will win and lose next year.
They name teams with closing
windows: Nats, Tigers, Blue Jays.
with aging stars and too many
free agents playing out contracts,

it's now or never for them.
After fifteen minutes, I browse
quickly through the channels,
find an old, almost forgotten film.

Last Monday, my doctor said
they needed to do a biopsy
on my new kidney. They found
protein in my urine, want to see
what could be going on in there.
They didn't seem too concerned,
mentioned possible treatments,
medication, steroids, the kind
that won't turn me into Barry
Bonds. I'm scared shit. I hoped
the transplant meant home free,
but the disease could be returning.
I am scarred from its past progression,
all the days spent on dialysis, how
bits of my life sifted through
my fingers like Spring wind.

I know anyone can die anytime,
especially me, but believed
my window had opened wider,
looked out further to watch myself
living a full life for a longer time
and I want to throw the window
wide open, turn into Peter Finch,
yell *I'm mad as hell and I'm not
gonna take it anymore*
or thrust my head out, take
the deepest breath ever, suck
and hold all the world inside me.

A GOOD MAN

At the end of our last phone call
my mom told me cousin Tom's
cancer came back. He's keeping
quiet about it, which everyone
will appreciate since he tends
to tell the same stories over
and over. Besides, somebody
will just say what can you do.
Someone else, it is what it is
and everybody will nod, think
he's seventy-five, how long
does he want to live anyway.
I like his Brooklyn Dodger
stories: the Duke of Flatbush,
Carl Furillo's canon arm, Campy
Jackie, Pee Wee and the way
his face would turn red, words
would spit out faster every
time my brother called them
the biggest chokers in baseball
history, losing so many world
series to the Yankees. Like smooth
jazz, he'd flow into talking about
the Mets, his Polo Grounds try out,
throwing to Choo Choo Coleman
in the bull pen, the call back
that never came, or that Sunday
when I was twelve and he pulled me
out of Mass because his softball team
needed a ninth body to avoid
a forfeit. He'd always make fun
of the three pathetic weak ass
dribblers I hit before bringing up
my over the shoulder catch in shallow
right that turned into the game-ender
when I spun around and doubled
the game-tying runner off second.

My mother coughs, wonders about
his forty year old, never diagnosed,
slow son and who will take care
of him now, while I remember
the month after my transplant,
how he sat in his car outside
my building, motor running,
waiting for the sun to show
its face, waiting to take me
for my twice a week, follow up
appointments, smiling like him
and his son were heading out
on his boat for a day of fishing.
When my mom says he's a good
man, my mind moves to Christmas
dinners, stuffing my face, trying
not to pick up the Italian bread
and smack him across the mouth
with it as he ranted about his tours
at the Two Six Precinct in Harlem,
the niggers, the spics, the way
they lived like animals, how
he'd leave the country, years
later, if monkey-man Obama
got elected. When my mom
notices my silence, she says
Tom would do anything for you.
I say, I know, I'll call him over
the weekend, see if there's
something I can help him with.

LAST SUPPER

Larry's on the couch, laid out
flat from the cocktail sedative
we gave him for this morning's
dental exam. Head back, mouth
hung open, he could be a closed
down coal mine or a dead relative
displayed in a bargain priced
coffin. I joke with staff to check
on his breathing while thinking
about his dementia, the way
it's shrinking his world, how
it won't be too long before
we're all standing, hands
folded, at the front of a Brooklyn
church, holding back tears
and then letting them fall
while Larry rests in peace.

These days, he just sits or lies
around doing nothing except
intermittently slapping his face,
banging his head or scratching
his neck while his moans haunt
the hallways. Staff supports
his every step as he struggles
from his bedroom to the bathroom,
the dining room to the TV room.
Still recognizing people, he grabs
their hand and opens his arms
for a hug that he hangs on to
like it's his life line. I feel shitty
when I slink away, mention paper
work I have to catch up with.
He's happiest when he's eating,
soft or chopped-up food he chews
with quick tiny chipmunk bites
and as soon as he's finished he takes
his thumb, points to his mouth

115

for more. We take him on special
weekly outings to Dunkin Donuts,
Mark's Red Hook Pizzeria, Ikea
hot dogs or always his favorite,
Burger King, where he seems
most like himself, light blue eyes
all lit up, waving to everyone,
laughing loudly. Our new worker
Janel gets a glimpse of all
she's missed and I am reminded
of who he was, how easily
he enthralled us all, how deeply
he snuggled into our hearts.

Larry came from the institution
thirty-nine years ago with half
of his teeth gone and the rest
rotting. Our nurse wrote a note
describing his present condition,
how eating is one of his last joys.
His new dentist filled out the clinic
visit sheet, typing he needed
to extract all remaining teeth,
something about an infection
getting into the blood, rushing
to his heart. If it were me,
I would rather go quickly
into the good night. No one
will ever know what Larry wants.
Even in his younger days, he never
could comprehend those kinds
of questions. The state-assigned
caseworker, the resident nurse,
his psychologist, and me will fill
out forms, present them in surrogate
court. Three or four strangers
will hand down a decision in less
than ten minutes. Either way,
when it's over we'll drive straight
to Burger King on Fulton and Larry
will eat like it's his last supper.

FINAL JOURNEY

Sitting in BB King's, finishing a burger
and fries, you wait for the house lights
to dim and bring Johnny Clegg on stage
for this tour he's called the final journey.
Cancer. You wonder how much he has left,
will he still tribal dance across the stage,
will his voice fill the room. A South African
super star who sells out stadiums, hardly anyone
you know knows his name. An ex-girlfriend
with two Peace Corps stints introduced you
to the seductive guitars, that chicken plucking
bass and soaring sax that make up his songs.
When the gale force of Clegg's vocals bled
into doo-wopping Zulu choruses that built
into battle cries, you were hooked. In and out
of prison for playing music with blacks,
he left teaching to bring his Scatterlings
of Africa around the world with his bands
Juluka and Savuka. Looking back, you think
about his long time dance mate assassinated
during the years of civil unrest, that video
when Mandela sashayed across the stage
with his big assed background singer, her high
piercing voice summoning the holiest spirits.

And tonight, it's all there. You're clapping
along, singing loud as you can, banging
the table, dancing in your white boy way.
Skin tingles, eyes water and with the music
lifting it's impossible to believe anyone's
ever going to die. Fuck cancer. You forget
that woman, the shitty things she's done,
how she's prohibited you from writing
about her autistic son and used your words
to keep you from visiting him. The songs
carry you further back in time: she's sitting
across the workshop table, blowing you away

with her first poem, her sharp blue eyes
brightening, growing fiercer as her words
build, explode, she's taking a half skip
and a couple of strides to meet you under
a movie marquee on Bleecker or waiting
at a back table in that Italian restaurant
on Thompson: cheap, good and not too
crowded with that sausage and peas sauce
you never got enough of, at the airport
in Portland as she wraps her arms around
your neck, stands on tip toes to give you
one deep kiss, a few soft, lingering ones.
She fits her arm in yours, leads you
to the garage, a quick drive to her bed,
until it's time to pick up her five year old
at school. You're not thinking about sitting
at your desk finding words to put on paper
to celebrate her son's life and everything
he still means to you. The music is beautiful,
joyful, as the moment Jesse opened the door
to his apartment and his mom still loved you.

ABOUT TIME

After my father's funeral mass,
friends and family gather
on the church steps to hug and cry,
complain about the priest's
African accent and how he knew
nothing about my father's life.
They give directions to the gravesite,
to our house, while I walk around
to the schoolyard. St Ann's school
has been closed for years
and the schoolyard seemed
so much bigger when I was twelve
and it was filled with hundreds of kids.
Girls in long lines rocking back and forth,
trying to find the right rhythm for jump rope,
skirts flying as they sprinted, leapt, floated
while I hoped to catch a hint of their panties
for a second or two. Circles of boys flipping,
scaling baseball cards against the wall.
I was always a first round draft pick
for punch ball, the only fifth grader
who could send a Pennsie Pinkie flying
over the roof. Down by the lunchroom rail,
Regina Rowland broke my heart
for the first time and showed me everything
wouldn't turn out the way I wanted
when she said that Tommy Schmidt
had already invited her to Rye Beach
and she didn't know how to tell him no.
Nuns in black habits took turns patrolling
the grounds like sentries, black beads
clicking, bouncing as they rushed to break up
a fight. The bell rang at 8:45 and everyone
froze until one of the sisters pinched her clicker
and we silently lined up in size place by class.
I walk back to the church, whisper something
to my youngest brother that makes him nod.

I put my arm around my mother, lead her
to the limousine, open the door for her.
I watch the altar boy kick the door stop,
pull the church door shut and see my father
on one knee telling me to smile, stand up
straight as he focused his Kodak camera
that muggy day in May when I made
Confirmation, became a man like him.
Tears fall out of my eyes and my sister
says it's about time I did some crying.

WHAT ANYONE KNOWS

Robert's twin sister calls
to tell me that their mom died.
I offer condolences, ask
when did it happen. Twenty
years ago, I'd see her
as she regularly visited
Robert at the group home
and I learned where Robert
got his sweetness, his warmth.
Recently, we'd drive him out
to Long Island for extended
weekend stays five, six times
a year. I'd sit at my desk, watch
his eyes light up as he blew sloppy
kisses and mumbled he loved her, too
on his weekly phone call. Joanne
wants to know what we should do
about Robert, the guy who was pulled
out of the womb after her. Diagnosed
with mental retardation and cerebral
palsy, he spent his early childhood
in Willowbrook hell. She wonders
how much of it he'd understand,
what would happen when he saw
his mom lying in the coffin, whether
he'd kick and yell, throw himself
on the floor when it was time
to leave, would he ever stop
crying. I wonder what anyone
knows about death, but tell
her I think he should go.
No one knows how much
Robert understands anything
since he can't tell you himself,
but I feel sure that sitting
in the church with the organ
mourning, the incense rising

121

as they close the casket
will be something he'll remember
whenever he goes home
to his family and never sees
his mom again no matter
how many times he asks
and he'll make some kind
of connection. I tell her
we'll put on his suit, sit
nearby and help him
with anything he needs,
and he'll get through
that day, the same way
he gets through his life.

LATE SUMMER SKY

After the transplant, the first
thing that enters my mind
when I wake up is no longer
what hurts most, what
will I be capable of doing
today. Before I step out
of bed, I whisper thanks
to my brother Jaime, stroke
my side where I believe
his kidney now resides.
My piss shoots out like new
a strong steady stream.
Standing there, still sleepy,
I begin thinking how to fill
the five hours I'd spend
at dialysis watching *Law
& Order* re-runs, fitting head
phones on and pressing shuffle
three days a week as I waited
for leg cramps to attack me,
my blood pressure to drop
like that Toots and The Maytals'
song. No need for afternoon naps.
I can now walk to the neighborhood
theater, sit and eat buttered popcorn
mixed with frozen Reese's pieces
while my eyes never leave
the screen through *Hell Or High
Water.* I go back to work, back
to a job I love that pays me more
than enough. And no, I won't
have to sell my Stub-hubbed
Brian Wilson tickets.

Tonight, I ride the subway, meet
Angelo for dinner in The Village.
We talk about the Yankees,

the silly, self important world
of poetry, that chump Donald
Trump. He tells me about his move
from down near the World
Trade Center up to Harlem,
the upstairs white lesbians
who help him with his laundry,
all the great Dominican food.
I ask about his long held
vegetarianism, he puts
a finger to his lips, blows
a quiet *sshh* and I smile.

I recite my updated health
report as I watch the door,
women escaping from a late
afternoon downpour, all wet
and wonderful. We give orders
to our waiter, pour water
from the bottle left on our table.
I tell him about all this time
I now have, wonder when
I'll start to feel lonely again.
I think about how long it's been
since I've been with a woman
wanting more than company,
conversation. Will I remember
the things I'm expected to say,
what to do if it ever gets
that far? Will it feel
like the first time, new, scary,
luscious? Will it feel anything
like love as I stare out the window,
watch the sky begin to darken?

CHEEZ-ITS

When the guy sitting next to me
realizes the stewardess gave him
the last pack of CHEEZ-ITS, he takes
his head-set off, offers me a few.
He was listening to Yo La Tengo
and I was in the middle of Dylan's
Series of Dreams. He saw Bob
with his parents when he was ten
and didn't know anything about
his music. I moved my hands like
Father Cunningham in the confessional,
forgave him. Visiting college friends
in Burlington, he's hoping for snow,
some skiing. I'm spending the weekend
with Jesse, my sort of step son. When
I get to the severely autistic part,
he doesn't bend his head to the side,
wince in a combination of pain and pity,
like some people do. He nods his head
and his eyes widen as this beatific smile
glistens across his face, as if he's come
across his first living, breathing saint.

I could try to explain how it feels
when Jesse opens the door, smiles,
and skips as if he would have died
if I knocked a minute past three thirty,
how everything is clear, completely
understood throughout our visit,
what and when we'll do things
written down like a map to treasure.
We ride the bus to Starbucks, eat
at the same restaurant. He orders
apple juice with ice, chicken fingers,
French fries, extra hot. Delighted
by cars driving alongside, the sights
we pass, people getting off and on,

he hums two word phrases, pops out
a burst of laughter now and again.
He makes a wounded bird sound
if we have to sit at the bar, wait
for a table or the waitress brings
his apple juice a bit too slowly
and he'll always send his food back
if he needs it *more hot please now.*

For three days, two nights, it's easy,
simple really, to leave myself behind,
the nonsense that usually bends
my thoughts with worry, doubt.
If Jesse was sitting next to me
instead of this philosophy professor
from Rutgers I could ask Jesse for a few
more CHEEZ-ITS and he'd tell me
the truth, answer *no,* or *one more,
that's it.* I wouldn't wonder if only
a greedy bastard like me would grab
the last one. I tell Phillip no thanks,
wave it off, when he extends the bag
my way and I decide not to say
anything else about me and Jesse.
I won't challenge the image of autism
tattooed into his brain and like everyone
who has nothing to do with it, he'll never
understand it. But really, nobody does
anyway. Besides, I don't mind being
his idea of a good person for the rest
of the flight. Three days, two nights,
one weekend a month, it's a blessing
to know I can help make someone I love
so easily happy and never wonder why
that never happens with anyone else.

THIS MONTH'S VISIT

After Jesse gives me the quick hug
I still have to ask for, he says *paper*
and walks to the table. I unlock
the room that's called the office,
come out carrying a blank sheet,
settle into my seat. He prints
September 6 2019 across the top.
I ask, *What should we do today?*
He always begins with the city bus
like he's spent either all morning
or his whole life waiting to ride
that bus into town and I feel
as if I'm fulfilling my one holy
purpose on earth helping to make
this guy happy. We continue down
the page: Starbucks, Blackbird
Books, a long slow Deerborn bus
loop where he asks to switch seats
at least twenty times and I shake
my head sideways, beg him to please
zip his lip as he laughs so loud
that everyone looks our way until
he moves closer, widens his eyes
and stares longingly into mine.
I am forced to say *okay, just once.*
He slides into a new seat, smiles,
then says, *change, one more please,*
while I make faces, act enraged.

We grab jackets, file out the door,
take the elevator and hit the street.
He walks fast, I move slow as shit.
He keeps looking back at me, down
the street, in case a bus appears
and we wind up trotting a few blocks
to catch it. But no, we can take it easy.
I start thinking about Brooklyn,

carrying Jesse out to the curb
for his first day of mainstream
schooling. With his six year old legs
wrapped around my waist, I felt
like his father. His mom aimed
a camera at us, juggled his backpack
filled with Winnie the Pooh books,
his lunch box stocked with Oreos,
Extra Spicy Doritos, the only things
he ate back then, and an index card
with all his information printed on it.
She was worried about the other kids
bullying him, laughing at his flapping
fingers, his constant percolating sounds,
his out-of-nowhere leaps of frustration
and delight. I knew he had no use
for other kids, wouldn't acknowledge
their existence unless things escalated
to physical cruelty. Jesse carries everything
he needs inside himself, stored beneath
his beautiful blue photographic eyes.
Sometimes, I try to be more like him.

We had driven a few practice runs,
repeated short simple phrases
while he looked out the car window,
hummed. We parked in front
of the school building, walked up
the steps, moved around back
and let him fly high on the swings.
Still, I'm not sure he knew where
he was going that morning, how
long he was expected to stay, what
they might try to make him do there,
or if he was afraid of not coming
back and ever seeing us again. When
the bus arrived, his mom lifted him
out of my arms, nuzzled his face
with swarming kisses that tickled him,

then finally placed him on the ground.
He walked up the steps casually,
that light bounce in each of his steps
as if he knew where he was going.
He found a window seat. We waved
until the yellow bus turned the corner.

Today, I lean in the doorway shade
of the nail salon. Jesse stands
ten feet away, sometimes taking
a quick little jump as cars flash by
or he turns to trace the lettering
in the shop's window and I try
to keep him from scraping it off.
Periodically, he walks over to me,
time please. I dig through pockets,
hand him my cell. Giving it back,
he says, *Friday October 4, come back,
two nights, Sunday October 6, go home,
Tony New York,* and I have to answer,
Yes, for sure or the whole world stops.
When the bus pops into sight, he skips
to the curb, bouncing on the balls
of his feet and waits for the door
to unfold. He drops five quarters
into the slot and walks down
the aisle like he owns the bus
and every single person on it.

OCTOBER

The woman in the jet blue seat
next to me is talking about
her weekend getaway. Every
year she leaves NYC behind
for fall in New England: a cabin
made of tree trunks, feeding
evening fires, ordering a stack
of pancakes soaked in fresh
tapped maple syrup, guys
in the next booth talking
Red Sox, Celtics and hunting,
two lane highways winding
deeper into woods, the explosion
of leaves, deep brush strokes
of colors, that breathtaking
blend and how no words
can touch their beauty.

No, I don't really give a crap
about her damn leaves
and wish I could say that,
strap headphones on,
get lost in my music.
Instead, I explain I'm going
to visit Jesse. He turned
twenty-two in June, graduated
high school. I saw photos
posted on line, his family,
his workers, surrounding him
at Buffalo Wild Wings and Jesse
laughing. I haven't seen him
since May. I told him I was sick.
My youngest brother gave me
a kidney and recovery was slow,
but I am moving much better now.
It was a prefect match
and my nephrologist said

I'll probably have to find
a different way to die.

He's an ex girlfriend's son
and I've known Jesse
since he was five. I decide
not to tell this woman he's autistic
thinking she can figure it out
if she listens. I describe
how good it makes me feel
when his worker drives him
to the airport. I ask for a hug
and he gives me one, always
hesitating before he wraps
his arms around me, tightens
his hold for a few seconds.
We do whatever he wants:
ride the city bus, eat sizzling
chicken fingers, French fries,
Ben and Jerry's brownies,
walk to the nearby bridge,
that park in Oakledge
to throw rocks into the lake,
and every minute or so
his eyes fill with delight
as if he has discovered
this amazing, messed up
world and the hidden
magic of its people
for the first time again.

Sometime, during my visit,
maybe when he's taking
a short or long break
at his apartment or riding
in the back seat, he'll lean
forward, tell his worker, *Tony,*
come October, two nights,
October 12. The worker

always tells him to talk to me
and Jesse repeats his question,
his demand, only a tick slower
as he stares into my eyes.
I nod, give him my promise.
Boarding my flight, I already
miss him. I feel a chill,
the distance between New York
and Portland growing wider
and I hear Jesse's request
singing in my ears like a mantra.

HOLIDAYS

When the guy next door,
yells out, *you think I'm happy*
the baby cries louder.
I am surprised not to hear
either of the dogs barking,
the wife cursing back.
I turn my music louder,
Laura Nyro's *Christmas*
Beads of Sweat for this New
Year's Day. I flew home
from visiting Jesse yesterday.
Nearly twenty years since
I spent New Year's Eve
with him, his mom. Happy.
I remember he was sleeping
and we were in bed. Straddling
my hips and laughing, small
town City Hall fireworks flashed
through the window, across
her eyes. The guy throws
a couple of fucks against
the wall and the woman
hits him with a son of a bitch.
These days we hardly talk.
Emails to arrange, confirm
monthly visits. We rarely
raised our voices, but the strain,
the silence, strangled the breath
out of the room. Something
bangs against the wall, shatters
across the floor. The husband
screams again. The Northeast
is frigid and that makes everything,
me, feel lonelier. Sometimes, I miss
Jesse's mom, even though I know
day to day we never fit that well.
A door slams and I hear footsteps,

paws, scuttling down the hall.
I love Jesse and miss him
as soon as I leave, but realize
how much easier my life has been
not taking care of a special needs kid
moment to moment. I walk
to the window, watch snow fall.
The woman next door's face
is hidden behind the hood
of her fur lined parka. She's trying
to pull the leash tighter, smoke
her cigarette, unfold a tiny plastic
bag and bend to pick up two
piles of dog crap before it stains
the new fallen snow. I go
into my bedroom and before
I close my eyes, I hear a lock
unlatch, the guy next door's
even tone, *Feel better now?*

THANKSGIVING

Sitting around the table,
everyone's staring at you.
No one has more reason
to be grateful than you.
Your youngest brother
gave you a kidney last July
and now you're dialysis
free, steadily reclaiming
parts of your life back.
You could tap your glass,
wait for quiet, lead everyone
in prayer and reach across
the table, plant a kiss
on Jaime's cheek. Luckily,
you don't do those kinds
of things in your family
and you've forgotten all
the prayers the nuns
forced you to memorize.

After surgery, your drowsiness,
that heavy anesthesia fog lingered,
faded slowly. You were in a bed,
a dark room. Your eyes darted
side to side, scanned the walls,
the ceiling, the light leaking
through the doorway. You slid
your hands up, down your body,
rotated your feet, clenched fists,
moved your head, left, right,
stretched your neck. All there
and in mostly working order,
you sunk back to sleep.

Others who had transplants
reported this immediate surge
of energy as if their whole being

was charged, a deep new breath
from the edge of a mountaintop,
the strength to lift a building
that collapsed on a frightened kid.
You never really believed that,
but were hoping to at least
open your eyes to a new world,
a wanderer waking to a distant
planet, looking for a new depth
behind every person's eyes.

But already your feet are fitting
into slip-on moccasins, stepping
onto your treadmill, riding
the F train to and from work,
clicking on lopsided Knicks games
when you get home, an occasional
movie, concerts now and then,
dinner with long time friends,
sharp stabs of loneliness,
sitting at your desk trying
to write something true,
struggling with everyday
worries, thinking, as always,
too much. All you can do
is reach for the alarm, lift
yourself out of bed, splash
water and wash the dreams
out of your eyes. Breathe in,
breathe out, take one footstep
after another, do what you do,
try to believe it's good enough.

GOOD

Walking in the neighborhood
Larry twirls like a circus bear
every twenty steps or so, bends
down and pulls up his socks
like Thurman Munson adjusting
his batting gloves before each pitch.
Lee walks down the aisle, sliding
his fingers along the packages
on every shelf, stopping to align
each one perfectly before he keeps
walking. Some kid stares and laughs,
another runs to his mother, eyes
wide with confusion. The mother
smiles at me, her face softens
into an apology and then crumbles,
turns into an *Oh you poor thing*
pitying pose. I look past her, move
closer to Lee, touch his arm, instead
of smacking the nice lady across
her mouth. I hold Robert's hand
as we walk through the park's gate.
He moves like a drunk Pinocchio,
nearly misses the bench as he stops
to sit. Jesse walks down the aisle,
plops down in a window bus seat
smiling widely as cars drive by,
humming his tuneless song, breaking
into loud laughter
                        and I'm five years old
again. Climbing onto the B55 bus
with my leg brace clanking, I drag
my huge booted foot through the crowd
as the people lean against poles,
grab hand grips. An old black woman
gets up, offers her seat to me.
My mom tells me to thank her,
but I whisper, *no thanks*, grab hold

of a pole and hang on, dream
about flying away, disappearing.
At home, I sit on the stoop, watch
some kids play stickball in the street.
A foul ball bounces my way. I catch it,
rub the Pennsie Pinkie as one
of the players runs it down. *"C'mon,*
give it back, you retarded gimp."
I extend my hand. When he gets near,
I tackle him, wrestle him to the ground.
Surprised, he tries to fight back,
struggle out of my hold. I kick him
with my brace. Red pours out of his head.
It felt good. It still feels good.

WHAT KIND OF MAN

The sliding wheels of carts
and the shuffling feet
of nurses coming down
the hall begin to open
my eyes. The light is still
shocking when they enter
my room. I turn away, bury
my eyes into the pillow
and listen to them talk
to the new patient
behind the drawn curtain.
When they ask about bathing,
he answers in a too loud voice,
*"Some things a man needs to do
for himself."* I'm next and I know
the nurse will have to help me
do everything and I start to think
how I got here. Just five years ago
I was walking from the subway
to my apartment, cutting through
the park on spring days, stopping
at the basketball court, maybe
loosening my tie, letting my shirt
flap out of its pants as I flew
down court, hung in the air
and double clutched my way
to the basket. After months
of accelerated kidney disease,
I started to hail cabs home,
slowly struggle my way
out the car door with a cane
to help me limp up the pathway,
wait for an elevator to carry me
up to 2B. When the nurse opens
my curtain, I tell him I feel a bit
better, but still weak. Breakfast
will soon be here and hopefully

my stomach can keep some of it
down. When he asks about bathing,
I tell him I'm all his and he goes
to get the basin and cloths. Not long
ago, I'd feel embarrassed showing
my private parts to anyone, worried
about size and how they would react
to being touched. After two operations,
I am over all that. Mostly, I am stuck
wondering what kind of man
I can still be? This morning,
I'm the kind of man who lets
a male nurse strip my clothes
to a pile on the floor, wash
my front and back, stand me up
and let me hold his shoulder
as he cups my balls, and gently
scrubs them clean while I try
not to inhale the tuna fish
on wheat he ate during
his late-night lunch break.
The kind of man who stares
at the wall and whispers
thank you into his ear.

The New York Quarterly Foundation, Inc.

New York, New York

Poetry
Magazine

Since 1969

Edgy, fresh, groundbreaking, eclectic—voices from all walks of life.

Definitely NOT your mama's poetry magazine!

The *New York Quarterly* has been defining the term contemporary American poetry since its first craft interview with W. H. Auden.

Interviews • Essays • and of course, lots of poems.

www.nyq.org

No contest! That's correct, NYQ Books are NO CONTEST to other small presses because we do not support ourselves through contests. Our books are carefully selected by invitation only, so you know that NYQ Books are produced with the same editorial integrity as the magazine that has brought you the most eclectic contemporary American poetry since 1969.

Books

www.nyq.org

poetry at the edge™

CPSIA information can be obtained
at www.ICGtesting.com
Printed in the USA
FSHW021722090720
71609FS